THE COMPLETE IDIOT'S GUIDE® TO

WITHDRAWN

Improving Your Credit Score

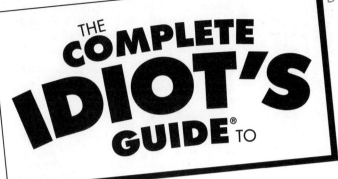

THE COMPLETE IDIOT'S GUIDE® TO

Improving Your Credit Score

by Lita Epstein, MBA

ALPHA

A member of Penguin Group (USA) Inc.

ALPHA BOOKS

Published by the Penguin Group

Penguin Group (USA) Inc., 375 Hudson Street, New York, New York 10014, USA

Penguin Group (Canada), 90 Eglinton Avenue East, Suite 700, Toronto, Ontario M4P 2Y3, Canada (a division of Pearson Penguin Canada Inc.)

Penguin Books Ltd., 80 Strand, London WC2R 0RL, England

Penguin Ireland, 25 St. Stephen's Green, Dublin 2, Ireland (a division of Penguin Books Ltd.)

Penguin Group (Australia), 250 Camberwell Road, Camberwell, Victoria 3124, Australia (a division of Pearson Australia Group Pty. Ltd.)

Penguin Books India Pvt. Ltd., 11 Community Centre, Panchsheel Park, New Delhi—110 017, India

Penguin Group (NZ), 67 Apollo Drive, Rosedale, North Shore, Auckland 1311, New Zealand (a division of Pearson New Zealand Ltd.)

Penguin Books (South Africa) (Pty.) Ltd., 24 Sturdee Avenue, Rosebank, Johannesburg 2196, South Africa

Penguin Books Ltd., Registered Offices: 80 Strand, London WC2R 0RL, England

Copyright © 2007 by Lita Epstein, MBA

International Standard Book Number: 978-1-59257-690-6
Library of Congress Catalog Card Number: 2007930859

09 08 07   8 7 6 5 4 3 2 1

Interpretation of the printing code: The rightmost number of the first series of numbers is the year of the book's printing; the rightmost number of the second series of numbers is the number of the book's printing. For example, a printing code of 07-1 shows that the first printing occurred in 2007.

Printed in the United States of America

Most Alpha books are available at special quantity discounts for bulk purchases for sales promotions, premiums, fund-raising, or educational use. Special books, or book excerpts, can also be created to fit specific needs.

For details, write: Special Markets, Alpha Books, 375 Hudson Street, New York, NY 10014.

Publisher: *Marie Butler-Knight*
Editorial Director: *Mike Sanders*
Managing Editor: *Billy Fields*
Executive Editor: *Randy Ladenheim-Gil*
Development Editor: *Nancy D. Lewis*
Production Editor: *Kayla Dugger*

Copy Editor: *Tricia Liebig*
Cover Designer: *Bill Thomas*
Book Designer: *Trina Wurst*
Indexer: *Johnna Vanhoose-Dinse*
Layout: *Brian Massey*
Proofreaders: *Aaron Black, John Etchison*

Contents at a Glance

Appendixes

Contents

Appendixes

Introduction

The three-digit number known as your credit score can greatly impact your ability to get credit and how much interest you'll have to pay when you get approved. That's not the only thing you have to worry about when thinking about that three-digit number. It can also hamper your ability to get a job and it can impact your insurance rates.

Yes, it's a powerful little number and how it's calculated is still a mystery. Luckily we know a bit about the results of that calculation and what you can do to improve it. We also know what you must avoid, so you don't send it into a downward spiral.

In this book, we explore what we know about how the credit score is calculated, what impacts the score, and what you can do to improve your score. We also show you how to read and correct your credit reports. Accurate credit reports are crucial to your ability to monitor the data that goes into the calculation for your credit score.

How This Book Is Organized

You'll start your exploration of the mysterious world of credit scoring by learning why it's important and how to read a credit report. Then you'll discover how to get a credit score and maintain it. Next we'll show you how to work your way through a credit crisis. Finally we'll show you how to avoid credit scams and identity theft and help you understand your credit rights.

We've organized the book into four parts:

Part 1, "Learning the Score," explains why you should care about your credit score and who controls the score. You'll also explore how to read your credit reports and how to fix them.

Part 2, "Maintaining Your Score," reviews the basics of getting and maintaining your credit score, and the importance of paying your bills on time, reducing your debt, and staying credit worthy. It also looks at the impact your credit score has on insurance rates.

Part 3, "Getting Through a Scoring Crisis," explores how to minimize damage to your credit score when facing a financial crisis, such as a job-loss, medical illness, or bankruptcy.

Part 4, "Avoiding Credit Score Mishaps," looks at what you can do to prevent ID theft and avoid credit score scams. You'll also find information about your credit rights and how to protect them.

Extras

I've developed a few helpers you'll find in little boxes throughout this book:

def•i•ni•tion

These will help you learn the language of credit reporting and credit scoring.

 Credit Cautions

These will give you warnings about things you need to avoid.

Scoring Surprises

These will help you explore additional information about key credit reporting and credit scoring topics.

 Scoring Tips

These will give you ideas for how to improve your credit score and manage your credit.

Acknowledgments

I want to thank my executive editor, Randy Ladenheim-Gil, for contacting me to write this very important book. In addition, I want to thank my development editor, Nancy Lewis, for her outstanding job of editing and keeping this project together. Also, I want to thank my copy editor, Tricia Liebig, for watching all those details.

Trademarks

All terms mentioned in this book that are known to be or are suspected of being trademarks or service marks have been appropriately capitalized. Alpha Books and Penguin Group (USA) Inc. cannot attest to the accuracy of this information. Use of a term in this book should not be regarded as affecting the validity of any trademark or service mark.

Part 1

Learning the Score

Why does a three-digit number known as your credit score have such a huge impact on your financial life? This part answers that question as well as others—who controls your score, how you can access the data that impacts it, and what you can do if that data is wrong.

Chapter 1

Why You Should Care About Your Credit Score

In This Chapter

- ◆ Defining the score
- ◆ Reviewing the types
- ◆ Mixing up the ingredients
- ◆ Computing your costs

Your credit score, which is just a three-digit number, wields incredible power over your financial life. A low credit score can cost you hundreds of thousands of dollars in interest over the years. You even could be stopped from getting a loan completely, if your credit score is too low.

In this chapter, I discuss the data behind that three-digit number and explain its impact on your ability to qualify for credit and negotiate the best interest rates for loans. Your credit score can even impact your insurance premiums and your ability to get a job.

What Is a Credit Score?

So what is this powerful three-digit number? The credit score is a mathematical analysis based on how you manage your credit. Credit scores assign a numerical value to bits of information in your credit report to calculate this number. Using this information they try to predict your financial behaviors in the future, such as whether you will pay your bills on time.

You may be surprised to find out that there are probably hundreds of credit scores out there, but the score used by most lenders is the FICO score, which stands for Fair Isaac Corporation—the granddaddy of credit scorers. A FICO score ranges from 300 to 850—the higher your score, the better your loan offers.

Scoring Surprises

The FICO score was first developed jointly by the Fair Isaac Corporation and Equifax (credit reporting agency) in 1989. Today it is the gold standard measure of credit risk used by more than 75 percent of mortgage lenders, as well as other financial institutions. The best credit rates are given to people with scores of more than 770, but 700 is considered a good score. The median score is 725. If your score dips below the mid-600s, the interest rates you'll be offered will be significantly higher. The figure on the following page shows what percentage of the population has various credit scores.

Lenders use a credit score to determine how risky it might be to loan money to you. If you have a high credit score, you are considered a good credit risk and you'll have access to lower interest loans. If you have a low credit score, you're considered a bad risk and you will pay higher interest rates to borrow money.

Insurers use the credit score because they believe there is a correlation between the credit score and the possibility that you will file a claim. Through study, insurers have found that people with a low credit score show an increased propensity to file claims. So if your credit score is low your insurance premiums are likely to be higher. I talk more about insurance and your credit score in Chapter 10.

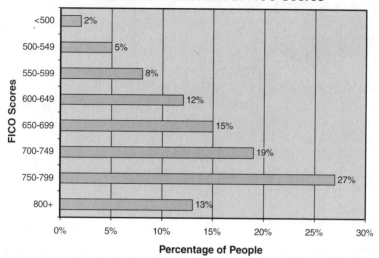

National Distribution of FICO Scores

FICO Scores	Percentage of People
<500	2%
500-549	5%
550-599	8%
600-649	12%
650-699	15%
700-749	19%
750-799	27%
800+	13%

Most people have a FICO credit score that falls between 650 and 799. In fact, you can see from the chart showing the "National Distribution of FICO Scores" that 61 percent of the population with a credit score has a FICO score in this range.

Exploring the Types of Scores

Although FICO is the granddaddy of credit scores, there isn't just one FICO score. There are actually six different FICO scores—two for each of the three credit reporting agencies (Equifax, TransUnion, and Experian). I talk more about the credit reporting agencies in Chapter 2.

The credit reporting agencies added to the confusion about credit scores by announcing the creation of the VantageScore, which is a new risk score developed through a collaboration of the three credit reporting agencies. By introducing this credit score the agencies hope to break the stranglehold Fair Isaac has on credit scoring and reap the financial benefits by selling their own scoring system.

When looking up your own credit score through one of the key credit reporting companies, you are likely to find one of the following three scores in addition to the VantageScore.

- ◆ BEACON—Equifax's version of the FICO score

- ◆ FICO Risk Score, Classic—TransUnion's FICO score

- ◆ FICO II—Experian's FICO score

In addition to these three scores, you may hear about Pinnacle (from Equifax), FICO Risk Score Next Gen (from TransUnion), or FICO Advanced Risk Score (from Experian). All three scores are part of Fair Isaac's newest scoring tool called NextGen, which Fair Isaac says is an advance in predictive technology, ordering consumers according to their likelihood of repaying their credit obligations. Using NextGen scores, Fair Isaac believes lenders can lower their bad debt rates yet increase their approval rates. Lenders are always looking for ways to increase their customer base and at the same time reduce their lending risk.

If you don't have an extensive credit history, Fair Isaac also has a credit score for you. Lenders can use a credit score called the FICO Expansion Score. This score is based on nontraditional credit data including public records, utility information, consumer or business credit information, and demographic information.

In addition to FICO and VantageScores, there are hundreds of smaller credit scorers out there that calculate credit scores for financial institutions, retailers, and other businesses that target specific consumer or business information more directly related to the risks the institution wants to measure. Some credit scores are designed to provide accurate risks for specific industries such as auto, bankcard, finance, and installment products. Others are globally based to provide an assessment of consumer risk in multiple geographic regions.

Not all scores focus on credit risk; some scores try to predict the likelihood that a customer will file bankruptcy. Equifax calls its bankruptcy predictor the DAS Bankruptcy Risk Model; TransUnion's is called Delphi Bankruptcy Risk Model Score; and Experian calls its bankruptcy scorer the CCN/MDS Bankruptcy Model Score.

Discovering the Components of Your FICO Score

How a credit score is calculated is a deep, dark secret that you probably will never get to see, but you can find out the bits of information that make up that credit score and how this information is weighted. All credit information is grouped into five categories: payment history, amounts owed, credit history, new credit, and types of credit used. The pie chart in the following figure shows you how these pieces are broken up.

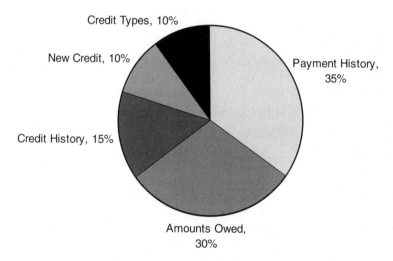

This pie chart shows how much weight various pieces of your credit background have on your credit score.

Different bits of information fall into each of these five pieces. Information about payment history, which makes up 35 percent of your score, includes the following:

♦ Payments you've made on your credit cards, retail accounts (such as Sears or Macy's), installment loans (such as a car loan), finance company accounts, and mortgages.

- Any adverse information in public records including bankruptcy, court judgments, liens, wage attachments, collection items, or other past due items.

- How much overdue your accounts are, if at all.

- How recent the items are on your account including past due items, collection items, or public record. For example, a five-year-old past due payment will not have as negative an impact on your credit score as a six-month-old past due payment.

- Number of past due items on your credit file.

- Number of accounts paid as you agreed to pay.

Information in the amounts owed part of the credit pie, which makes up 30 percent of your score, include the following:

- Total amount you owe.

- Amount you owe on each account.

- Number of accounts with balances.

- Proportion of your credit lines used. For example, whether you've used 30 percent or 80 percent of your credit available in an account.

- Proportion of any installment loans you still need to pay.

The length of credit history, which makes up 15 percent of your score, includes the following:

- Time since your accounts were first opened.

- Time each specific account has been opened.

- Time since there was activity on the account.

Information about new credit, which makes up 10 percent of your score, includes the following:

- Number of accounts you opened recently and what proportion of your accounts are new accounts.

- Number of recent *credit inquiries*. These relate to inquiries made by creditors to who you've applied for new credit.

- ◆ Time since your last credit inquiry.

- ◆ If you had payment problems in the past, the amount of time since you started reestablishing a good credit history.

def•i•ni•tion

> **Credit inquiries** include any request by a third party to look at your credit report. There are two types of inquiries—hard and soft. A hard inquiry is one based on an application you filled out when applying for credit. A soft inquiry is one where a creditor looks at your file possibly to offer you a new credit card or to look at the credit history of you as a current customer.

The final 10 percent of the pie relates to the types of credit used. This includes the number of different types of credit accounts you have as well as their prevalence. The credit scorer also looks at the most recent information on each type of credit. Credit types include credit cards, retail accounts, installment loans, mortgages, consumer finance accounts, and any other type of credit you may have.

These bits of information are given a numerical value that fits into a set of mathematical equations, which are designed to predict your future payment behavior. Analysts have devised these mathematical equations based on patterns noticed in millions of bits of data. Lenders believe your credit score based on this predictive mathematical model indicates the likelihood of your behavior regarding the use of credit in the future.

As the old adage goes—garbage in, garbage out—if the information in your credit report is not accurate, your credit score won't reflect your likely behavior. Your score might be lower than it should be just because the data being input is wrong. That's why it's important to review your credit report and make sure it's accurate. I talk about how to read your credit report in Chapter 3 and how to correct it in Chapter 4.

What a Low Score Costs You

Why is it important to keep that three-digit number accurate and as high as possible? Your cash flow depends on it. During your lifetime you could end up spending hundreds of thousands of dollars extra on interest if your score remains low.

In the following table, I show you the impact a FICO score has on the interest rate you'll be charged and the cash payments you'll need to make based on those interest rates.

FICO Score Impact on Your Interest Rates and Payments

FICO Score	Interest Rate on $175,000 30-Year Mortgage	Payment on Mortgage	Interest Rate on $50,000 15-Year Equity Line	Payment on Equity Line	Interest Rate on $25,000 60-Month Car Loan	Payment on Car Loan
720–850	6.081%	$1,058	8.472%	$492	7.142%	$497
700–719	6.206%	$1,073	8.772%	$500	7.947%	$506
675–699	6.743%	$1,134	9.272%	$515	9.467%	$525
620–674	7.893%	$1,271	10.047%	$539	11.101%	$545
560–619	9.843%	$1,515	11.547%	$586	14.486%	$588
500–559	10.581%	$1,611	12.797%	$626	15.128%	$596

The rates shown here were the national averages in January 2007.

You can see that a person with a top FICO score between 720 and 850 would be charged a 6.081 percent interest rate on a 30-year mortgage with a monthly principal and interest payment of $1,058. A person with a lower score in the range of 500 to 559 would be charged 4.5 percent more in interest (10.582 percent) and his monthly payment would be $553 higher.

Yikes. Yes, the difference in the amount you will pay based on your credit score can be tremendous. The numbers I show are based on the national average interest rates available in January 2007.

Scoring Tips

Fair Isaac has an excellent calculator you can use to view today's interest rates based on credit scores and how your payments will be impacted. You can input your loan amounts and the calculator will automatically calculate the differences based on credit score. You can try out this calculator at www.myfico.com/myfico/CreditCentral/LoanRates.asp.

To give you an idea of how your credit score can impact what you are able to spend during your lifetime, I developed the chart in the following figure. You can see that a person with a top credit score of 720 to 850 will spend an average $270,000 less on interest than a person with a low score of 500 to 559. That leaves the person with a higher credit score a lot more money to spend on other things.

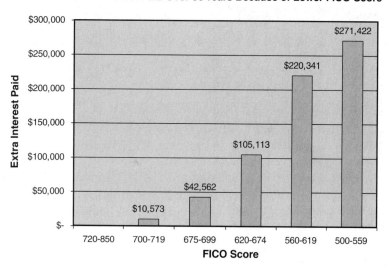

This chart shows how much extra interest a person with a low credit score would have to pay during a 30-year period. The chart was developed using Fair Isaac's calculator.

In developing this chart based on a 30-year financial lifetime, I included a 30-year mortgage of $175,000, two 15-year equity lines of $50,000, and four car loans of $25,000. So in actuality the interest paid during a lifetime would be even greater. When one throws credit cards into the mix, interest costs can soar. Credit card interest rates for those with the best credit scores can be as low as 7 percent to as high as 29.99 percent for people with a poor payment history.

Take the time to find your credit score and work to improve it so you can get the best interest rates. Each credit reporting agency has its own version of the score, so a good place to compare what you've got is www.myfico.com. You can get a free copy of your credit report once a year from each of the credit reporting agencies at www.annualcreditreport.com/cra/index.jsp, but you will have to pay for your credit score.

If you're one of those people who must have the highest score on everything, don't look for perfection in your credit score. A FICO score of 770 or higher will always get you the best interest rates and loan offers available. Even credit reporting agency spokespeople will tell you they haven't seen a perfect credit score of 850 for anyone. The high usually tops out at 825.

The Least You Need to Know

◆ Your three-digit credit score impacts whether you can get a loan and how much interest you'll pay.

◆ The accuracy of your credit score depends on what is in your credit report.

◆ Keeping your credit score as high as possible can save you hundreds of thousands of dollars in interest during your lifetime.

Chapter 2

The Who, What, When, Where, Why, and How of Credit Reporting Agencies

In This Chapter

- ◆ Exposing the agencies
- ◆ Figuring out who furnishes the data
- ◆ Contemplating the credit report users
- ◆ Meeting the Big Three

You know how important that three-digit credit score can be to your financial life, but who controls that number and how do they do it? Three multi-billion dollar credit reporting agencies, that make money on the information collected about you, control the data used to calculate your credit score.

In this chapter, I explain what credit reporting agencies are and how they operate. Then I talk about the companies that furnish information to the agencies and finally discuss who uses the data collected. After you know these basics, I explore each of the Big Three credit reporting agencies: Equifax, Experian, and TransUnion.

Exploring Credit Reporting Agencies

So what is a credit reporting agency? I take that definition right out of the federal law that governs these agencies—the Fair Credit Reporting Act—"... any person which, for monetary fees, dues, or on a cooperative nonprofit basis, regularly engages in whole or in part in the practice of assembling or evaluating consumer credit information or other information on consumers for the purpose of furnishing consumer reports to third parties, and which uses any means or facility of interstate commerce for the purpose of preparing or furnishing consumer reports."

So the two key activities of credit reporting agencies include the following:

- Collecting public record information plus consumer account information.

- Providing the information collected to third parties.

Although other reporting agencies exist that provide information on a regional basis for specific business or commercial reports, employment background, check approval, or screening of tenants, only the Big Three do so on a national basis. In fact most of the specialty agencies use the core information from one or more of the Big Three to develop their own reports.

Because the core of credit reporting is confined to the activities of the Big Three, I focus this chapter on how they operate. If you want to improve your credit score, you'll have to concentrate on correcting any erroneous data in the reports generated by the Big Three.

Following the Data Furnishers

All the information collected by the Big Three is stored in data warehouses. The data is furnished by your current and former creditors, as well as service bureaus. Service bureaus are agencies that scan public record information.

Feeding the Credit Data Beast

Creditors feed the beast—the data warehouses of the Big Three—with information about your personal history (collected as part of your credit applications) including your date of birth, employment information, and address history in addition to information about your credit activity, credit status, maximum credit line, payment history, delinquencies, and collection activity.

Creditors subscribe to one or more credit reporting agencies so they can both pull reports on a consumer, as well as report credit information about their customers. Creditors pay fees for both reporting information and for running credit checks. So the credit reporting agencies make money by both collecting data and giving out the data collected.

Why would a creditor pay money to report your credit history? Creditors have found that a negative credit report is one of the best ways to collect from you. Most people will clean up a negative report by paying off the debt involved (even if they dispute the amount), if they are applying for a loan to make a major purchase, such as a new home.

Service bureaus provide information that they find at courthouses and county offices including court judgments, bankruptcies, liens, and any criminal records. Service bureaus provide a service to the credit reporting agencies. They are paid for that service.

The credit reporting agencies also store data regarding any inquiries about your credit file and the type of inquiry—whether a soft inquiry (usually used to check the payment history of existing customers or for marketing new credit cards) or a hard inquiry (when you apply for new credit and a creditor checks your credit history).

Dangers of Default

You may wonder why creditors would check your payment history on other credit lines after they've already offered you a credit card. Most credit card agreements today have a dastardly clause called the *universal default clause*, which states that if you are late on another credit card, your interest rate can be increased on the credit card you have with the company checking your credit history.

For example, if you have credit cards with MBNA and Citicorp and you make a late payment on your MBNA card, the late payment will show on your credit report. When Citicorp does a soft inquiry to review your payment history on your Citicorp card, even if you haven't been late on any payments with Citicorp, Citicorp could increase your interest rate to the maximum if your credit card agreement includes the universal default clause.

That's why it's important to monitor and correct your credit report at least every six months. Even if you have a legitimate dispute pending with a credit card company, if a late payment or nonpayment is shown on one of your credit reports, all your credit cards with the universal default clause could increase your interest rates based on that report. South Dakota and Delaware, where most of the credit card companies are based, have no caps on interest rates allowed. That's why you'll see interest rates as high as 32 percent on some cards if you are considered in default. The Supreme Court has ruled that interest rate rules are set on a state-by-state basis and the laws of the state in which the credit card company is located or the state in which the credit decision was made stand if the interest rate is questioned.

Credit Cautions

To protect yourself, be certain you dispute all your credit problems in writing with every credit reporting agency that shows the error and save copies of all letters you send as well as all responses. If a company jacks up your interest rate based on negative credit information on another account, you'll need to prove that you have a problem with that specific credit account, but that you are not a credit risk. In the credit game you are considered guilty until you prove yourself innocent. I talk more about the dispute process in Chapter 4.

Understanding the Users of Credit Reports

Who can use your report? Users of the credit reports generated from the data warehouses of the Big Three include individuals, businesses, agencies, or other institutions that want to determine your credit worthiness. In addition, some businesses pull your credit history if you are being considered for employment and some insurers pull your credit history as part of the underwriting process to decide whether to insure you and how much to charge.

Users also could be marketers for the credit card companies and other financial institutions that are looking for potential customers based on a certain credit history. You know all that junk mail you get offering credit cards, car loans, and mortgage loans? The marketers most likely got your name culling potential customers based on a search of the data warehouse of one of the credit reporting agencies.

You might think that a credit report sits there waiting for someone to request it. Well that's not what happens. In actuality, the data about you sits in the data warehouse along with the data of millions of other consumers. When someone wants to use the services of a credit reporting agency and requests a credit report about you, the credit report is generated.

The user must provide specific identifying information including your name, date of birth, exact address, current and former employers, and Social Security number. If the user does not subscribe to the service of the credit reporting agency (pays a monthly fee to access consumer data), then the information must match exactly.

But most credit card companies and other subscribers to credit reporting agencies can get away with less complete information. For example, a subscriber can get a consumer's credit history even if they only have seven digits of the Social Security number. These searches also allow differences in the spelling of a person's last name or address. These less-than-perfect searches often result in credit reports with inaccurate data, especially if your data matches another with a similar name and Social Security number. You certainly can expect to experience more problems with this less-than-perfect matching if your last name is Smith or Jones or some other common name versus someone with a more unique last name such as Kirschenbaum.

Another common problem is when a father and son or mother and daughter share the same name. Often their credit reports become merged and it can take years to sort out the problems, especially if you're the one with perfect credit and your mother, daughter, father, or son has a poor credit history.

Your credit history could be perfect, but if someone with a similar last name or Social Security number has a terrible credit history, you might be fighting an uphill battle every time you apply for credit. If you've already experienced a problem with erroneous information showing up on your credit report because you have a common last name, mention that up-front when applying for a major loan, such as a mortgage. Your loan officer will know to look for that and help you sort through the problems. Remember the loan officer only makes money if he succeeds in closing your loan, so often he can advise you about how to develop written information to prove your case with the lender.

Who Are the Big Three?

So now that you know what the Big Three do, let's take a closer look at who they are and how they make their money. Later on in this chapter I detail Equifax, Experian, and TransUnion, but first let me discuss some key points that are true about all three.

One thing you can be sure of is that they don't care about you. All they care about is making money. Even if you subscribe to one of their monthly services for the purpose of monitoring your credit report, you're just chump change to them, but they may be a little nicer if you try to correct a report than they are to consumers who don't subscribe. In fact if you do subscribe, you're given a different customer service number than nonsubscribers to correct any errors. But all corrections will need to be requested in writing with written proof of anything you think is wrong. Always remember you are considered guilty until you prove yourself innocent.

Credit reporting agencies would be even happier if they weren't required to allow you access to your credit report. That requirement was made mandatory by the Fair and Accurate Credit Transactions Act (FACTA) passed into law in December 2003. So to make the best of a bad situation, the credit reporting agencies try to make a little bit of money by selling credit monitoring services. Now, don't take this wrong. I do think credit monitoring is a good idea and I talk more about that in Chapter 3. But don't think that you become a true moneymaking entity for the credit bureau. Their profits come primarily from their true customers—creditors and other users and furnishers of their information.

Scoring Tips

The Fair and Accurate Transactions Act (FACTA) was passed by Congress in December 2003. The Act mandates that you receive a free copy of your credit report from each of the Big Three to help you stop identity theft. The Big Three don't make it easy to find out about this free copy and even hide its availability on their primary consumer websites. They've collaborated and now provide one website to order all three, as long as you can find it. Don't order a free credit report from anywhere other than www.annualcreditreport.com/cra/index.jsp. All other websites promoting free reports are usually selling some type of credit monitoring service.

You are primarily a thorn in the side of the credit reporting agency, especially if you are a good credit consumer and challenge any erroneous information on your report. The credit reporting agencies do make some money on your purchases of credit monitoring services, but that is usually short-lived profit. Most people who monitor their credit report become pests because they want to be sure their report is accurate.

Every time the credit reporting agencies have to deal with you to correct information they actually lose money, because they must pay staff to work on the corrections rather than generate new moneymaking activity. If you threaten legal action, you may get a quicker response—as long as you know your legal rights and use them appropriately. I talk more about that in Chapter 18.

Be aware that credit reporting agencies can shut down your credit report in response to a lawsuit, so use that option cautiously. If your report is shut down, a creditor who wants to check your report will get the message, "file under review," which can make it impossible for you to get credit. If this happens to you, let your attorney know immediately and he can respond to this attempt at intimidating you.

Equifax

Equifax boasts that its information assets include 5 billion *credit trade-lines*, approximately 50 million commercial files, and 310 million consumer demographic and lifestyle profiles. In addition to this database, Equifax develops applications to process data in various ways to

def•i•ni•tion _____

> **Credit tradelines** include details about a specific credit account. For example, if you had an account with Citigroup, your credit tradeline would include all the account information about that specific credit card including your credit limit and payment history.

help its clients make decisions about potential future customers, as well as increase the profitability of current customers.

When you get a notice offering you an increased credit limit or additional credit cards, it's usually because Equifax or one of the other credit reporting agencies ran a program and identified you as a good prospect for more credit based on criteria set by the requesting lender that wants to offer a defined group of potential customers new credit. Remember credit card companies only make money when you purchase on credit and then pay interest on that credit. In fact, people who pay off their cards every month are the ones called deadbeats by the credit companies.

Equifax's 2006 revenue totaled more than $1.3 billion with more than 4,600 associates in 13 countries. Their business operates through three segments—Equifax North America, Equifax Latin America, and Equifax Europe.

In addition to providing credit monitoring services to consumers at www.econsumer.equifax.com, Equifax's biggest moneymakers offered to business customers include the following:

◆ Equifax Small Business Credit Risk Scores—Provides business credit reports, credit scores, and portfolio analysis to help customers find their high-growth segments.

◆ TargetPoint Acquisition—Provides prescreening for marketing new products.

◆ FirstSearch—Services collections professionals and helps them find debtors.

◆ Fraud Solutions—Works with the European government, law enforcement agencies, and industry to identify and help prevent fraudulent activity.

◆ Government and ID Verification—Works with the British government to develop a system to verify the identities of passport candidates and make it more difficult for criminals to obtain false documents.

◆ Experto—Provides customized decision and scoring applications that can be used by banks, telecommunication companies, and other businesses (developed specifically for the Latin American market).

Experian

Experian Group Limited, which was founded in 1955, is based in Dublin, Ireland, and listed on the London Stock Exchange. It employs more than 12,500 people, operates in 30 countries, and supports customers in more than 60 countries. Its annual revenues exceed $3 billion.

In addition to the credit monitoring services it offers to consumers at consumerinfo.com, Experian's primary lines of business include the following:

◆ Credit Services—Assists businesses in making credit decisions to lend profitably to other businesses and consumers.

◆ Decision Analytics—Helps businesses make decisions to minimize credit risk, provide fraud protection, offer better customer service, and provide account management.

◆ Marketing Solutions—Helps its customers acquire new customers and builds more profitable relationships with current customers.

TransUnion

TransUnion started as a railcar holding company in the 1960s, but quickly moved into the business of providing intelligence about consumers. In 1969, TransUnion acquired the Credit Bureau of Cook County (Illinois), which maintained 3.6 million card files manually in more than 400 seven-drawer cabinets. Today the company operates in more than 30 countries, employs more than 4,000 people, and provides services to 50,000 businesses worldwide. The company processes 2.1 billion pieces of data each month. Because it's a private company, no income data must be reported to the public.

In addition to offering credit monitoring services for consumers at www.truecredit.com, the key services TransUnion offers to its business customers include the following:

◆ Fraud Response Services—Assists companies with protecting their customers and their business by providing solutions in the event of a data breach or identity theft (both short-term and long-term solutions).

◆ Marketing Services—Helps companies identify new markets so they can reach the best potential prospects.

◆ Risk Management—Provides data to assist companies with taking advantage of new opportunities while reducing their risk exposure.

◆ Collections Management—Provides systems to help companies improve their collection rate through prioritizing their accounts for collections, and helps them locate delinquent customers.

The credit reporting agencies control all the key information about your financial life. Get to know your credit reports and the agencies that prepare them.

The Least You Need to Know

◆ Credit reporting agencies collect information about you from creditors and service bureaus and then make that information available to third parties who want to determine whether you are a good credit risk.

◆ Lenders are not the only ones who use the credit information collected by credit reporting agencies. Insurers and employers also commonly use the information.

◆ The Big Three credit reporting agencies—Equifax, Experian, and TransUnion—are multi-billion dollar companies that not only collect credit information and provide credit reports, they also provide this information to marketers who want you to accept even more credit.

3

Getting to Know Your Credit Report

In This Chapter

- ◆ Getting your reports
- ◆ Verifying your identity
- ◆ Navigating the negatives
- ◆ Checking on who's checking you out
- ◆ Exploring your accounts
- ◆ Starting to monitor

Your credit report is like a snapshot taken on a particular day and time of your financial and personal life. If all the information is accurate, then it should factually reflect your outstanding credit, your payment history, the status of your credit accounts, and any information that can be found in public records.

I indicate that it's similar to a snapshot because the same information pulled just a few days later could vary depending on when your creditors report their data about you each month. If you happen to pull your report just before a monthly update, your credit balances may not accurately reflect your financial history as of the day the information is pulled. For example, suppose you made a payment on December 15 and the credit card issuer reported your balance as of December 14, your credit report would not show the payment as made until the next report on January 15.

In this chapter, I review the key parts of a credit report then show you how to read any codes you might find. After you become familiar with the report, I discuss how important it is for you to monitor that information.

Ordering Your Credit Reports

Before reading this chapter, I recommend that you order a set of your credit reports so you can review your information as I discuss what you will find in them. If you haven't ordered your free report this year, you are entitled to one free report from each of the credit reporting agencies—Equifax, Experian, and TransUnion.

The fastest and easiest way to get those free reports is by using their cooperative online website at www.annualcreditreport.com/cra/index.jsp. You can order your free report and receive it in less than a minute from any of the agencies by answering a few identifying personal questions. Each agency asks different questions but all will ask for your name, address, and Social Security number. Other questions will likely involve some recent credit activity.

If you are uncomfortable with the idea of accessing the information online, you can request your free annual credit report by calling 877-322-8228. You can also request your reports by mail using the form shown in the following figure, which you can download at www. annualcreditreport.com/cra/requestformfinal.pdf. The completed form should be mailed to:

Annual Credit Report Request Service
PO Box 105281
Atlanta, GA 30348-5201

If you order the report by phone or mail, it will probably take two to three weeks to show up in your mailbox.

EQUIFAX   experían   TransUnion.

Annual Credit Report Request Form

You have the right to get a free copy of your credit file disclosure, commonly called a credit report, once every 12 months, from each of the nationwide consumer credit reporting companies - Equifax, Experian and TransUnion.
For instant access to your free credit report, visit www.annualcreditreport.com.

For more information on obtaining your free credit report, visit www.annualcreditreport.com or call 877-322-8228.

Use this form if you prefer to write to request your credit report from any, or all, of the nationwide consumer credit reporting companies. The following information is required to process your request. **Omission of any information may delay your request.**

Once complete, fold (do not staple or tape), place into a #10 envelope, affix required postage and mail to:
Annual Credit Report Request Service P.O. Box 105281 Atlanta, GA 30348-5281.

Please use a Black or Blue Pen and write your responses in PRINTED CAPITAL LETTERS without touching the sides of the boxes like the examples listed below:

Social Security Number:

Date of Birth:

Month   Day   Year

Fold Here   Fold Here

First Name   **M.I.**

Last Name   **JR, SR, III, etc.**

Current Mailing Address:

House Number   **Street Name**

Apartment Number / Private Mailbox   **For Puerto Rico Only: Print Urbanization Name**

City   **State**   **ZipCode**

Previous Mailing Address (complete only if at current mailing address for less than two years):

House Number   **Street Name**

Fold Here   Fold Here

Apartment Number / Private Mailbox   **For Puerto Rico Only: Print Urbanization Name**

City   **State**   **ZipCode**

Shade Circle Like This → ●

Not Like This → ⊗ ∅

I want a credit report from (shade each that you would like to receive):
○ Equifax
○ Experian
○ TransUnion

○ Shade here if, for security reasons, you want your credit report to include no more than the last four digits of your Social Security Number.

If additional information is needed to process your request, the consumer credit reporting company will contact you by mail.

Your request will be processed within 15 days of receipt and then mailed to you.

31238

Copyright 2004, Central Source LLC

If you want to request your free credit reports by mail, use this request form. You can download a copy at www.annualcreditreport.com/cra/requestformfinal.pdf.

You can get a copy of your FICO credit score as well, but you will have to pay for that. When you order your free report you'll be given an option to buy your FICO credit score. You may be offered another type of credit score. Most lenders use the FICO credit score, so you may want to get the real McCoy at www.myfico.com rather than from the credit reporting agencies. I talk more about how to order your FICO scores in the later section, "Importance of Credit Monitoring."

Checking Your Identifying Information

When you do get a copy of your credit reports the first thing you should check is the personal information section. You'll find the primary name for which you ordered the report followed by a list of one or more former names. Women may have a particularly long list if they have been married several times.

Your Social Security number should not be shown in its complete form. You may find your number shown as a series of Xs (XXX-XX-XXXX) or you may find it partially shown, such as 123-44-XXXX. This is for your protection and safety.

Next you should find your current address followed by a listing of previous addresses. Be sure all the addresses shown correspond to addresses that you have had. If you find erroneous addresses listed, it probably means that someone else's credit information has been merged with yours and you'll need to scour the report to find all the erroneous information. You have a mess to clean up, but it will help your credit score if you do—especially if the erroneous information is negative (meaning a lot of late payments and past due accounts or possibly even a bankruptcy).

The next section lists your employment history. Check to be sure the information accurately reflects your employment. Again the listing of a job you never had could be an indication that someone else's credit information has been merged with yours.

Digging Into the Negatives

Hopefully you won't have any negatives, but if you do, it will be in the Negatives section on the report. This section can include derogatory public records, collections, and late payments or other problems.

Derogatory Public Records

If you filed for bankruptcy, owe money because of a court judgment, lost a house to foreclosure, had your wages garnished, or have a Federal tax lien on your record, then you will find the information in this section of the report.

In the detail section you will find the following:

Type of Record—Bankruptcy, tax lien, judgment, foreclosure, or garnishment.

Court Number—If appropriate.

Amount—Amount of money involved.

Date Filed—Date the public record was initially filed.

Status Date—Date the status was last updated.

Date Reported—Date of the last report about the record.

Scoring Tips

A bankruptcy will stay on your credit report for 10 years, but its impact on your FICO score will be low when it's at least three years behind you. Paid tax liens and judgments also have a reduced impact on your FICO score after three years. So if you're rebuilding your credit score after a rough financial period the longest you must wait is three years for decent interest rate offers as long as you pay all remaining bills on time and don't take on too much credit.

Most negative information will be removed from your credit report in seven years. A current or recent late payment will impact your score much more than a bankruptcy after it's been discharged for more than three years. I talk more about how to clean up negatives in your report in Chapter 4 and about your credit rights in Chapter 18.

Collections

Any time you don't pay your bills on time and the creditor turns over your account for collections to a third party, the information about the collection appears in this section of the credit report. Information you'll find about these types of accounts includes the following.

Collection Agency—The agency that is handling the collections.

Original Creditor—The creditor that turned the account over to the agency.

Account Number—A partial number, such as 12345XXXX.

Whose Account—The person or people who are on the account. If you're the only one on the account, it will say "Individual Account."

Date Assigned—The date the collection agency was assigned the account.

Date Reported—The last date the agency received a report about the status of the account.

Amount—Amount to be collected.

Balance—Balance still owed. This amount could be higher than the original amount because interest and fees will continue to be added to the amount due.

Date Paid Out—Date you paid the collection or the collection was charged off.

Date Closed—Date the collection was closed.

Late Payments and Other Account Problems

Any accounts for which you made a late payment will be listed in this section. The information is usually presented in a column format:

Account Type—Types can include revolving, installment, overdraft/reserve checking, or mortgage.

- ◆ Revolving account includes credit card accounts and retail store accounts. Essentially these are accounts where your balance due can go up and down depending on how much you charge.

- ◆ Installment accounts include car and furniture loans. These are accounts where you agreed to pay a specific amount during a specific period of time until the full balance is paid off.

- ◆ Overdraft/reserve checking accounts are accounts where the bank automatically draws from your allowable credit if you write a check for more than your balance. These types of accounts allow you to avoid overdraft fees on checks.

♦ Mortgage accounts include any loan in which you put your house up as collateral, which means the lender can take your property if you don't pay the loan.

Company—The company to whom you owe the money and a partial account number.

Current Status—This could include paid or paying as agreed, debt discharged through bankruptcy, account transferred to another office (usually collections), charged off as bad debt, or unrated.

Worst Delinquency—This could include 30, 60, or 90+ days past due, collections, *charge off*, or bankruptcy.

Negative Description—You will usually see a yes or no in this column with a link to details following the column.

def•i•ni•tion
> **Charge off** means that the creditor wrote off the account to bad debt and does not expect you to ever pay the money.

Review all the information in the negative section very carefully for accuracy. If the information is accurate, there isn't much you can do but wait it out. The good news is that even the worst of the negative information will not have a major impact on your credit score when you are at least three years past whatever caused the negative mark.

Most negative information will be completely removed from your credit report in seven years. I talk more about how long the negative information will appear on your report and how you can challenge it in Chapter 4.

Reviewing Credit Inquiries

Another section of your report will be called Inquiries. In this section you'll find information about lenders or other interested parties, such as a utility company, who have viewed your report. The first list of inquiries, which includes the date of contact and the company that requested your information, are the hard inquiries. These are inquiries by companies to whom you have applied for credit.

Some reports will include a second list of inquires called soft inquiries. This list will only be given to you and not to other creditors checking your report. The soft inquiries are companies that pulled your credit history either for marketing purposes or to review your credit activity if you already have an existing account. This list will include the creditor and date of inquiry.

Credit Cautions

If someone is trying to use your credit identity for the purposes of identity theft, one of the first alerts you'll receive is a credit inquiry from a creditor to whom you did not apply. I talk more about identity theft, how to prevent it, and what you should do if you suspect you are a victim in Chapter 17.

In addition to the two inquiry lists, you'll also get detailed contact information for each company that requested to see your credit in case you want to contact them for more details about why they asked to see your report. If you see creditors with whom you are not familiar and to whom you never applied for credit, it is wise to contact them to find out why they checked your report.

Examining Listed Accounts

The fourth section of the report will be a listing of your accounts. At the top of this section is a summary of your accounts and then detailed information about each account follows. In the summary you will find the following:

◆ Number of accounts.

◆ Number of accounts with balances.

◆ Number of accounts that are negative, which includes late payments, late fees, collections, bankruptcies, foreclosures, and repossessions.

◆ Total balance on all accounts.

◆ Length of credit history, which dates to the oldest account you have on file with the credit reporting agency.

After the summary will be a list of all accounts in a summary table format with columns detailing ...

Account Type—Revolving, installment, overdraft/reserve checking, or mortgage.

Company—The creditor.

Date Opened—The date the account was first opened.

Negative Items—This will be either a yes or no and there will be a link for more information if you've accessed the report online. Otherwise you'll find the detailed information in the next section of the account section where all accounts are detailed individually.

When you view the information about each individual account you'll find the creditor's address and phone followed by these details:

Account Number—This should not be a complete number. It should be a partial number followed by Xs.

Type of Account—Revolving, installment, overdraft/reserve checking, or mortgage.

Monthly Payment Terms—Such as the amount of an installment or mortgage payment or the minimum monthly amount due.

Date Opened—The date the account was first opened.

Date of Last Activity—This could include a new charge or new payment, depending on which activity is the most recently reported to the agency.

Date Paid Out—Date paid in full or charged off.

Date Closed—Date the account was closed, if applicable.

Loan Type—This could include credit card, automobile, charge account (retail account such as a gas company or department store account), VA real estate mortgage (home loans for veterans guaranteed by the Veterans Administration), FHA real estate mortgage (home loans guaranteed by the Federal Housing Administration), conventional real estate mortgage (the majority of mortgages in the United States), home equity loan, and line of credit.

Collateral—Whether the account is guaranteed against an asset. For example, whether your home is put up for collateral against a mortgage (if you don't make your payments, your home can be taken from you).

Description—Any detail that the creditor wants to add to describe the account's status, such as transferred to collections, charge off, and so on. Carefully review all the details about each account to be sure they are accurate.

Payment History—The payment history will include month-by-month details about how you pay your bills. Symbols will be used to show your history. Each credit reporting agency uses its own set of symbols. For example, for Equifax a * represents pays or paid as agreed. You want to see all *s. Other symbols include: 30 (30 to 59 days past due), 60 (60 to 89 days past due), 90 (90 to 119 days past due), 120 (120 to 149 days past due), 150 (150 to 179 days past due), 180 (180+ days past due), CA (collection account), F (foreclosure), VS (voluntary surrender), R (repossession), and CO (charge off).

Importance of Credit Monitoring

I can't emphasize enough how important it is for you to regularly monitor your credit report. At the very minimum you should request a copy of your report every six months. You not only need to review your report for accuracy, but you also want to find out if someone else might be using your identity.

If you see items on your credit report that you don't recognize, quickly call the creditors involved and find out more detail about the accounts. The faster you stop someone from using your identity, the easier it will be to clean up the mess. In Chapter 17, I talk more about protecting your credit identity.

Each of the credit reporting agencies offers monthly credit monitoring, where alerts are sent to you by e-mail if there are any major changes to your report. This includes new accounts, new account inquiries, and major changes in balances. You can set the alert levels for all the warning messages. For example, if you want to be alerted whenever your credit balance changes by 20 percent, you can set that as a warning. Or if you want to know whenever your balance changes by $500 or more you can set that as a warning.

To access these credit monitoring services you must go to each credit reporting agency's website:

◆ Equifax: www.econsumer.equifax.com

◆ Experian: www.experian.com/identity_fraud

◆ TransUnion: www.truecredit.com

All offer a number of different monitoring packages from which you can choose.

You may also want to consider the monitoring service from myfico. com, which is run by the credit scoring agency Fair Isaac. In addition to monitoring changes to your Equifax report, you also get alerts about changes to your FICO score. This service is called ScoreWatch, and you can get a 30-day trial for free at www.myfico.com/products/ scorewatch/freetrial.aspx. MyFICO also offers a package deal where you can order all three credit bureau reports with your credit score.

Scoring Tips

A cost-effective way to keep track of your credit is to order your free copy from each of the bureaus once a year. Then order the myFICO package of all three reports six months later. That way for a total of $47.85 ($42.84 if you commit to automatic annual repots from myFICO) you can check your credit reports twice a year plus check your FICO scores annually.

The Least You Need to Know

◆ Order your credit reports for free once a year.

◆ Check your personal information, any negatives, all inquiries, and account information for accuracy.

◆ Inaccuracies could be a sign of identity theft or the merging of your credit history with someone else's.

◆ Monitor your credit report at least twice a year. That way you can correct any problems before they turn into a negative that hurts your credit score.

Chapter 4

Dealing with Report Errors

In This Chapter

- Erasing credit errors
- Challenging reports
- Disagreeing with credit denials
- Dealing with public record problems
- Understanding "do-not-confuse" statements

Everyone faces problems with their credit reports at some time in their life, whether it involves a charge that is incorrect on your credit card bill or a negative mark on a credit report that is not based on what truly happened.

These negatives can result in a "no" decision on future credit, even if the negative mark is not a true reflection of your credit history. In this chapter, I talk about how to correct errors either on your accounts with your creditors or on the reports generated by the reporting agencies. I also discuss what your options are if your credit application is denied.

Correcting Credit Errors

I would be surprised if you never experienced an error on your credit card bill. Common errors experienced almost every month by someone who has a credit card include charges never made or charges that differ from the amount you agreed to pay. It's important for you to take steps to correct these errors as quickly as possible to avoid a negative report to the credit reporting agencies, which will impact your credit score.

You have 60 days from the date you receive a billing statement to dispute a charge. If you do find an error in billing within that 60-day window, you will find information on the back of your credit card bill telling you how to challenge the bill. The information will usually be in very small print, but the section with the details usually starts with something such as, "In Case of Errors or Questions About Your Statement ...."

Scoring Tips

You may find it difficult to correct errors if the charge is for future travel that isn't scheduled until after you're outside the 60-day window. If you do pay for travel in advance, be certain you are working with a reputable travel company because your right to challenge that charge will be lost after the 60-day window expires. Some credit cards allow you to challenge a charge for as long as 12 months. If you frequently charge future travel, look for a credit card that gives you a longer window to challenge a charge.

Follow those instructions carefully to protect your credit rights. (I talk more about your credit rights in Chapter 18.) Although you can call your credit card company to discuss the problem, you will also need to notify the company in writing to protect your rights.

def•i•ni•tion

A **charge back** is the process for disputing charges to your credit card bill. You must dispute a charge on your bill within 60 days after you receive the bill or you will not be able to use the charge back process.

When you dispute a charge the process is called a *charge back*. During the dispute period you are not responsible to pay the amount due and you should not be charged interest on the outstanding amount due. The merchant involved has the responsibility to prove that you did make the purchase and the amount of that purchase. That doesn't mean, however, that you shouldn't supply information to help prove your case about the disputed charge.

You should attempt to clear up any error with the merchant first. Sometimes it's truly a glitch in the merchant's computer system. I know I've found that charges can be made twice in a row because of a computer glitch and the merchant will quickly issue a credit. That credit can take a couple of billing cycles, so you should also dispute the charge with your credit card company directly to avoid any interest charges while you are waiting for the credit to appear on your bill.

Often a credit card company will instruct you to fill out a "Notification of Disputed Item" form or a "Description of Error" form. You can access this form on your credit card company's website or you can call your credit card's customer service number and they will send you a form.

I include a copy of Citicorp's "Notification of Disputed Item" form in Appendix C. The key information you'll need to complete on these forms includes the following:

- ◆ Name
- ◆ Account number
- ◆ Amount of dispute
- ◆ Date of transaction
- ◆ Merchant name
- ◆ Reason for dispute
- ◆ Your signature

In the "reason for dispute" section of the dispute form, the credit card company will usually have a place for you to check off the reason for the dispute and leave you blanks to fill in the critical details. Here are some common reasons for dispute on Citicorp's form, but they are common to many credit card dispute forms.

If You Did Not Make the Charge

You will check a statement such as, "Neither I nor any person authorized to use my card made the charge listed above. In addition, neither I nor anyone authorized by me received the goods and services represented by this transaction."

If you check this statement, you are indicating fraudulent use of your credit card and you should call your credit card's customer service number immediately, if you haven't already done so. Customer service will likely transfer you to the fraud division and you will be asked to complete a fraud report by telephone. You will also be sent a report form you'll need to complete in writing. I talk more about credit fraud and scams in Part 4.

Amount Billed Reflects Transactions You Did Not Make

If you *did* charge a purchase with the merchant, but additional purchases you did *not* authorize have shown up on your billing statement, then you should check a statement such as, "Although I did participate in a transaction with the merchant, I was billed for _____ transaction(s) totaling $_____ that I did not engage in, nor did anyone else authorized to use my card. I do have all my cards in my possession. Enclosed is the authorized sales slip."

This too could be a sign of fraudulent use of your card and you should call your credit card's customer service number if you see transactions you did not authorize, even if you did buy something at that merchant's establishment. You likely will be asked to file a fraud report when this type of billing error is seen.

Did Not Receive Merchandise You Ordered

If you never received merchandise you ordered, you should check a statement such as, "I have not received the merchandise that was to have been shipped to me. Expected date of delivery was _____ (mm-dd-yy). I contacted the merchant on _____ (mm-dd-yy), and the merchant's response was _____ _____."

Scoring Tips

A good general rule to follow when you order on the Internet is to only order from websites that provide a toll-free number for customer service. Try to call that number and ask questions from a customer service person before ordering. That way you can judge for yourself how customer-friendly the company is. Also, be sure to find out where that merchant is located. If you take the time to check out the merchant, you'll save yourself lots of headaches after you place an order.

These types of complaints are happening more and more often as more and more people buy things on the Internet. If you use a credit card for an Internet purchase, be certain you know the merchant or have some contact with the company prior to ordering.

Returned an Item

If you returned an item after you purchased it, you should check a statement such as this: "I have (select one) ___ returned ___ canceled the merchandise on _____ (mm-dd-yy) because _____ _____ _____."

You will be asked to provide a copy of the returned receipt or postal receipt to prove you returned the item. If you mail something back to a company, take the time to go to the post office or a mail service store and get a receipt for the shipping that permits you to track the package and provides you with proof of delivery.

Have a Credit Slip

If you returned the item and have a copy of the credit slip, you should check a statement such as, "I was issued a credit for $_____ on _____ (mm-dd-yy), which was not shown on my monthly statement. A copy of my credit slip is enclosed."

Be very careful when you get a credit slip and place it near where you pay your bills. That way it will remind you to watch for the credit on your bill. If the credit doesn't show up on your bill, you will have the proof you need for your credit card company.

A Credit Was Shown As a Charge

Occasionally an error will be made when a credit, which was supposed to be subtracted from your bill, is actually added to the amount due. If this happens, you should check a statement such as, "The attached credit slip was listed as a charge on my statement."

When you send in the form, attach a copy of the credit slip you have.

Merchandise Was Damaged During Shipping

Sometimes you will receive the merchandise ordered, but you receive it in damaged condition. When this happens, you should check a statement such as, "Merchandise that was shipped to me arrived damaged and/or defective on _____ (mm-dd-yy). I returned it on _____ (mm-dd-yy). Merchant's response was _____

_____

_____. I have provided the postal receipt and/or credit slip."

As I said, whenever you return an item to a merchant be sure you can prove that you did return that item and can show it was delivered to the merchant. You can do that by using a postal service that provides package tracking or by sending a package through the post office and paying for "return receipt requested."

Amount Charged Was Incorrect

If you find the amount charged to your account is different than what you expected, you would check a statement such as, "My account was charged $_____ but I should have been billed $_____. Enclosed is a copy of the sales receipt and/or other documents which indicate the correct amount."

With this type of error it is important to send a copy of the original, signed charge receipt. That will strengthen your case.

Credit Cautions

If you are someone who does not keep credit card slips until you get your bills, start doing so now. You will have a hard time questioning the amount of a charge without the receipt, especially if a disreputable person changed the amount after you left the store or restaurant. For example, this can and does occasionally happen in a restaurant when a waiter adds a tip that you did not authorize.

If the error you see is not reflected in one of the choices offered to you on the dispute form, then you should write a letter describing the error and attach it to the completed dispute from.

Sometimes when something starts as a billing error it can end up as a negative mark on your credit report, if your creditor reports you as paying the bill late while you are in the middle of a dispute. If this happens you should dispute that negative mark immediately both with the credit card company involved and with the credit reporting agencies. Late payments can hurt your credit significantly. I talk more about the impact of late payments in Chapter 7.

Disputing Report Errors

In Chapter 3, I talked about all the parts of a credit report and what type of credit information is important to correct. Here I discuss the process for seeking those corrections.

The first step in the correction process is to send a written letter to the credit bureau listing any errors you found, what is wrong with the information on the credit report, and how you think the information should be corrected. I include a sample letter to a credit reporting agency in Appendix C.

Here are some common problems and how you should ask for a correction:

Inaccurate name—Indicate which name on the list of names for you is incorrect. Correct the spelling of the name. If the name is one that you have never used, state that and ask that it be removed.

Account that is not yours—If you see an account listed that you have never opened, indicate which account and the account number. When this situation exists you will not have a full account number and can only give the partial number listed on the report. State that you have never opened the account and that it should be removed. In this situation you also should contact the creditor involved and be sure someone has not opened an account using your identity. If you find that your identity has been used to open an account, then you will need to report identity theft. I talk more about that in Chapter 17.

Account is listed more than once—If you find that the same account is listed more than once, indicate that and ask that the credit bureau only list the account once.

Spouse's account on your report—If one of your spouse's accounts is listed on your report and you are not a cosigner of that account, indicate that you are not responsible for the account and that it should be removed from your report. This can be especially critical if your spouse is not good about paying his bills on time. That can create a black mark on your otherwise good credit and hurt your credit score.

Payment history not accurate—If your report shows a late payment for which you were not late, indicate that you did not pay late and ask that the information be corrected. You should include the creditor's name, account number, and late payment or payments being questioned. If you have a canceled check or other proof of paying on time, send that along with your dispute. Ask the credit reporting agency to correct any inaccuracies.

Incorrect balance—If your account shows an incorrect balance, you should ask for the correction. But if the balance that you are seeing on the report is one that was correct 30 to 60 days ago, it may just be that the record has not been updated for the month involved. You can indicate the correct balance in the letter you send and if you have a recent statement showing the balance, it doesn't hurt to send a copy of your statement. This becomes critically important when you are trying to improve your credit score. You get your best score when all your accounts have only 10 percent or less of the credit used. For example, if you have a $1,000 credit line, the account looks best when your balance is $100 or less. So if the credit reporting agency is showing a $900 balance even though you've paid most of it off, you can improve your credit score by getting this updated.

Past due account—If your credit report shows that you have a past due account, but you are caught up on all your bills, you should indicate which accounts are paid in full and ask for the credit reporting agency to report the account as current.

After you send the letter, the credit reporting agency has 30 days to respond to your letter and indicate how it will handle your challenges to the report. In that 30-day period the agency will investigate your claims and contact the creditor that reported the information. If you have supporting data to prove your claims, it's best to send that along with your letter. In most cases the agency will believe the creditor unless you have solid proof the creditor is wrong.

When you get the response from the reporting agency, you may still disagree with what the creditor is reporting. In that case, you need to contact the creditor directly to correct any inaccuracies.

You have 60 days to correct the information from the time you receive a response from the credit reporting agency. During that period if you are not satisfied with the response of the creditor, you

Scoring Tips

If you still disagree with the information that has been verified by the credit reporting agency, you have the right to submit a brief statement in writing indicating the nature of your dispute. The statement you submit will become part of your credit report and will be disclosed each time someone asks for the report.

can then contact the credit reporting agency again. In the response letter that you get from the credit reporting agency, you will get detailed information about how to ask for an additional investigation.

Any time a request for investigation of your credit file results in a change to that file, you have the right to ask that the corrected report be sent to any company that requested the information in the past six months. If you live in California, Colorado, Maryland, New Jersey, or New York, you can ask that the credit report be sent to any company that requested the information in the past 12 months.

Sometimes a potential or current employer gets a copy of your credit report. If the entity that requested a report was a current or potential employer, you can ask that a newly updated and corrected report be sent to any company that requested a report in the past two years.

I talk more about your credit reporting rights in Chapter 18.

Handling "No" Decisions

Why should you care so much about every little detail on your credit report? Two reasons: your credit score and your desire to get approval for future credit.

If you get a "no" decision when you apply for credit, the creditor will send you a letter indicating why you were denied credit and which credit reporting agency supplied the information. You will also be given instructions regarding how you can request a free copy of your credit report from the credit reporting agency involved.

Always take advantage of that free report if you are denied credit, even if you don't intend to question the "no" decision. Use that opportunity to look at what is on the report and correct anything that you find to be inaccurate.

In most cases, you probably will not try to question the "no" decision. It's much easier to correct anything inaccurate and just apply for credit from another source. But this will not be the case if you are seeking a mortgage or other major purchase. If the "no" decision is based on something inaccurate in your report or something you believe needs to be explained, don't just accept the "no" decision.

For example, if you are denied a mortgage for a home you are planning to buy, talk with the mortgage broker and see if there is any way to salvage the deal. Often a mortgage broker can help you explain a negative report to the satisfaction of the mortgage company's underwriting department. If not, the broker may be able to help you find another lending source for the mortgage.

Public Records

If you find something inaccurate in public records, you should include that in any letter you send to the credit reporting agency asking for corrections. In addition though, you should contact the county where the records are inaccurate and ask for a correction to be filed to correct the public record.

For example, if a lien was placed against your property and you paid off the underlying debt related to that lien, take the information proving you paid to the county office where the lien was placed. Show the information that you have and the county staff will help you clean up the record. County clerks assist people with resolving problems to their public records every day.

You will find most of them willing to help you. If not, contact an elected county official and let them know the problems you're having getting help from their staff. After you have cleaned up the public record, you can then send a letter to the credit reporting agencies asking them to correct your credit report.

"Do-Not-Confuse" Statements

Sometimes you may find that your credit report includes the credit history of someone other than you. This can happen if you have a common name or if two or more people in your family share the same name. You will need to send a letter explaining the inaccuracies and ask that the affected accounts be removed from your report.

In addition to that you should send a "do-not-confuse" statement and ask that you are not confused with the same party again. In your "do-not-confuse" statement you should include any information you may have about the other party included on your report, such as name, address, phone number, place of employment, and any other identifying information you know.

"Do-not-confuse" statements are most effective if both parties involved send statements. If you know the other party, ask them to also send a statement indicating not to confuse your records. If you don't know the other party, but have a way to contact them, try asking them to send a "do-not-confuse" statement and give them the key information they need about you that they can put in the letter.

Take the time to check out your credit report at least twice a year and clean up any inaccuracies. You'll be glad you did when you next apply for a mortgage, car loan, or other credit account. You'll have a higher credit score and be able to get more attractive interest rates with a clean, accurate report than you will with one that has a lot of negative errors. I talk more about the things you can do to boost your score in Chapter 11.

The Least You Need to Know

♦ If you find something wrong on your credit report, don't hesitate to write the credit reporting agency and ask them to correct the problem.

♦ When challenging information on your credit report, send any information you have to back up your claim.

♦ If you get a "no" decision in the mail that results in a denial of credit, don't just accept it. Get a free copy of your credit report and correct any errors.

◆ Any errors on public record must be corrected by the county clerks where the record was originally recorded. Ask the county clerks for advice on how to best clean up a problem. Be sure to bring any proof you have of the error when you go to the county clerk's office.

◆ If your credit file has been merged with someone else's, file a "do not confuse" statement with the credit reporting agencies.

Chapter 5

Busting the Credit Score Myths

In This Chapter

- ◆ Closing accounts and lowering credit limits
- ◆ Checking credit and rate shopping
- ◆ Having payment in full and statements on file
- ◆ Getting credit counseling and bankruptcy

Lots of myths float around regarding how you can get the best credit score. Others talk about how to destroy your credit score. Many of these myths are totally untrue and the score is actually impacted in a way opposite of the myth.

In this chapter, I deflate those myths and tell you the real score.

Myth 1: Closing Accounts Can Help Your Score

When you apply for a mortgage, you might be told by your lender that you have too many accounts open and if you close some accounts you'll have a better credit score. Well, it doesn't quite work that way and if you do close one of your older accounts you might even hurt your credit score.

Basically, credit scoring rewards people who use their credit wisely. As long as you pay your bills on time and don't rack up balances to the max on all your revolving credit cards, your score won't likely be hurt by having a lot of unused credit lines. The best scores go to those people who use their available credit moderately and responsibly over a long period of time.

There are two reasons why closing your accounts could hurt your score:

◆ If you close your older accounts, the remaining accounts will make it look like your credit history is younger than it really is. If you do apply for a mortgage and the lender says you must close some credit cards as a condition to getting that mortgage, be certain to close the more recent cards rather than ones you've had for many years. Closing older accounts can definitely hurt your credit score.

def•i•ni•tion _____

Debt utilization ratio looks at the amount of debt versus the amount of available credit. It is calculated using this ratio: debt/total credit.

◆ When you close accounts, the amount of credit available to you will be reduced and the percentage of debt used versus available credit will soar. That _debt utilization ratio_ could make you look like more of a credit risk and your credit score could actually go down.

For example, suppose you had $600 in outstanding charges on your credit cards. You had three credit cards, each with a $2,000 credit limit totaling $6,000 of available credit. In this scenario your debt utilization ratio would be 10 percent (600/6000). You get your best credit score if you keep your debt use at 10 percent or lower of available credit.

Now suppose your lender asks you to close one of those credit cards. Your credit limit would now total only $4,000. Your debt utilization ratio would then increase to 15 percent (600/4000). Your credit score likely would drop if everything else on your credit history remained the same.

If you are asked to close your credit lines to get approved for a mortgage, do so, but do so carefully. Be sure to close the newest accounts and leave your oldest accounts open. Your score may go down for a short period of time, but it's worth it to get the house. After you've closed on the mortgage, you can fix the problem by paying down existing debt to reduce your debt utilization ratio or by opening a new credit card later if you need or want the credit.

I like to pay my bills in full each month and not carry anything over on a credit card. The interest rates are just too high. If you can get yourself into that practice, not only will your credit score soar, your financial situation will be healthier.

You also may want to close some credit cards if you don't use your credit wisely. For some people credit can be like an addiction. They tend to spend to their limit on every card. Not only will that get you in trouble financially, it will also reduce your credit score dramatically.

Myth 2: Lowering Your Credit Limits Can Help Your Score

Lowering your credit limits definitely will not help your credit score; instead this request will likely hurt your credit score. Essentially the reason for this involves your debt utilization ratio. Just as with closing accounts, the amount of credit available to you will go down and your overall debt utilization ratio will go up.

Much better than lowering your credit limits is to make a goal of paying off your debt so your debt utilization ratio goes down. Any

> **Scoring Tips**
>
> You can overdo it if you have too much credit available. Each time you apply for a new credit card, your credit score likely will go down, so be cautious about getting too much credit.

time you increase the gap between your balance and available credit it has a positive effect on your credit score.

Myth 3: Checking Your Credit Report Can Hurt Your Score

You will not hurt your credit score by asking for a copy of your credit report, as long as you do so directly and don't ask a friend at the bank to do it for you. When a bank or other financial institution requests a credit report, it gets tracked as a hard inquiry and the credit reporting agency sees it as an application for new credit, which will hurt your score.

You definitely should check your credit report from each of the credit reporting agencies at least once a year to be sure the report is accurate. I talked more about how to do that in Chapters 3 and 4. To quickly catch any sign of identity theft it's better to check your report at least twice a year.

Scoring Tips

MyFICO and each of the credit reporting agencies sell monthly alert services to let you know whether someone has checked your credit report or opened a new account in your name. You can also get an alert if the balance on any of your credit cards has changed dramatically. These services do a good job of alerting you to possible fraud and giving you the opportunity to correct the situation before it becomes a major problem. You can try the one offered by myFICO for free at www.myfico.com/SystemAccess/MyProducts.aspx. This service offers both monitoring of your credit report, as well as your credit score, for $8.95 per month.

Myth 4: Shopping for the Best Credit Rates Can Hurt Your Score

A slick salesperson might tell you that if you shop around for the best credit rates you can hurt your credit score. Anyone who tells you that is giving you a snow job to get you to sign on the dotted line quickly.

Anytime you go shopping for rates within a short window of time, FICO lumps these requests into one inquiry. For example, suppose you applied to four different mortgage lenders to find the best rates and these applications were all made during a two-week period. FICO would pick this up as shopping for rates and would lump all four requests into one and count it as just one hard inquiry against your score.

You don't want to drag out the process of applying for a major loan though, such as a mortgage or car loan. You should try to make your applications over a short period of time (two weeks or less is best) to minimize the risk that the hard inquiries would be seen as individual inquiries rather than being lumped into one.

You also don't want to apply for a car loan or a new credit card just before applying for a mortgage. If you apply for new credit lines that are not related to the same purchase, your credit score will go down. When applying for a mortgage, which you'll be paying over 30 years, you definitely want to get the best interest rate. You do that by having the highest credit score.

By priority—and the most difficult to get—is a mortgage loan. If you are thinking of buying a house, check your credit report, clean it up, and then apply for the loan. You should start the cleanup process at least 90 days before you apply for that mortgage loan because it takes time for any corrections to be made and your credit score to be adjusted. I talk more about cleaning up your credit report before applying for a major loan in Chapter 11.

Also, don't give your financial details to anyone until you are actually ready to buy. Car dealers especially are notorious for checking your credit history even before you sign a contract to buy. Those inquiries will show as hard inquiries, which is the same as if you applied for the loan, even if you never signed an offer to buy at the dealership. Those hard inquiries will hurt your score even though you didn't even open a line a credit.

Hard inquiries will hurt everyone's credit score. If you have excellent credit a hard inquiry will hurt less than if you have poor credit. Any time you're trying to rebuild your credit score, don't apply for any new loans until you know your score is improved.

While you're waiting to improve your score, the best things you can do are pay down your existing credit lines on time and improve your debt utilization ratio. Then when you do apply for loans in the future you'll be able to get the best rates.

Myth 5: You Must Pay in Full to Get a Good Score

You don't have to pay down all your credit cards to zero to get a good credit score. In fact using your cards occasionally and showing that you make all payments on time can give you a higher credit score than someone who never carries a credit card.

The credit score looks at how you handle credit over time. So even though you may prefer to have no credit at all and work solely on a cash basis, that too can hurt you. If you don't buy on credit and pay for everything with cash, you'll likely have a low credit score. Though it may not matter to you if you don't intend to apply for credit, it could impact your insurance rates.

Yes, insurance underwriters do look at your credit score. They believe people with low credit scores tend to file more claims. Some states have banned insurers from using credit scores to set a person's rates. I talk more about credit scores and insurance premiums in Chapter 10.

Myth 6: Putting a Statement in Your File Can Improve Your Credit Score

If you've been battling it out with a creditor and don't want to pay a bill, you could end up with severe damage to your credit score. Although the law requires that credit reporting agencies allow you to submit a statement of explanation when you dispute a negative mark on your credit report, these letters are not coded and used to calculate your credit score.

Lenders who ask for a credit report will get the attached statement, but many credit decisions are made purely on the score with no one ever looking at the statement. So even though the letter may be in place, your credit score could still be damaged by a past-due bill sent to collections.

If the amount in dispute is a small enough amount that you can pay it off without financial distress, your best bet would be to pay off the amount in question and take the vendor to small claims court to get a refund. Why hurt your credit score because of a $30 or $50 dispute with a utility company or other small vendor?

Myth 7: Credit Counseling Hurts Your Score More Than Bankruptcy

Don't believe this myth for a second. The worst thing you can do to your credit score is file Chapter 7 bankruptcy; the filing will stay on the credit report for 10 years. A Chapter 7 bankruptcy is where all your debt is discharged and the creditors are never paid.

Credit counseling will not impact your credit score. The current FICO formula ignores any reference to credit counseling. In fact, credit counseling is seen as a neutral factor when a credit history is scored. It doesn't hurt your score, but it also doesn't help it.

But this doesn't mean that your credit score can't get hurt if you enter a credit counseling program. Some creditors report you as a late payer even if you have enrolled in a debt management plan with a credit counselor. Others will put a notation on your credit file indicating that you are participating in a credit counseling program.

> **def•i•ni•tion**
>
> **Credit counseling** is a process where counselors who specialize in negotiating lower interest rates work out payment plans with your creditors to help get you out of debt. The plans they work out are called *debt management plans.* I talk more about credit counseling and how it works in Chapter 13.

It's true some lenders see credit counseling as a Chapter 13 bankruptcy, but after you've successfully completed a credit counseling plan the information will be dropped from your credit report, whereas a Chapter 13 bankruptcy can be reported for seven years. A Chapter 13 bankruptcy is where you pay at least part of the debt you owe to your creditors during a three- to five-year period.

Myth 8: Bankruptcy Makes It Impossible to Get Credit

Although it's true that bankruptcy does destroy your credit at least temporarily, it's not true that you can never get credit again. In fact, you may not even have to wait that long.

But you will have to expect higher interest rates on any credit for which you apply after the bankruptcy. Initially your score will be so low that you have great difficulty getting any credit, but in a year or two you should be able to ease the black mark if you pay all remaining bills on time.

Immediately after bankruptcy the only type of credit card you'll likely be able to get is a secured credit card, which is one that requires you to maintain a balance in a savings or checking account that matches the credit line. Your interest rate will also be high because you are considered a *"subprime" borrower*, which means you are high risk. You also will likely have to pay annual fees to keep the card.

def•i•ni•tion

A "subprime" borrower is one that has less than perfect credit. A bankruptcy definitely puts you in this category, but you can also end up there if you have a lot of late payments, repossession (major items taken back for nonpayment), or a foreclosure (house taken back by lender) on your record. "Subprime" borrowers must pay interest rates at least 5 to 10 percent higher than borrowers with a better score. I talked about the difference in interest rates in Chapter 1.

If you find you need to file bankruptcy, be ready for a long struggle to get back to the point where you can get decent interest rate offers. However, that doesn't mean you can't buy a car or a house. In fact some lenders think someone who files for Chapter 7 bankruptcy and can't file again for eight years is less of a risk than someone who still has other debt to pay off.

The key is to find a lender willing to take the risk at the lowest interest rate offer possible. Initially you may have to take a credit card with the maximum interest rate. Use it sparingly and pay it off on time every month. In about a year, you'll find lenders more willing to offer better credit rates with a card that has lower fees or maybe no fees at all.

As long as you proved that you can handle credit responsibly after a bankruptcy by paying all your bills on time, you probably will find a lender willing to take the risk on a car loan or mortgage about two to three years after declaring bankruptcy. But do expect to pay higher interest rates than others with a good credit score.

The Least You Need to Know

- ◆ You won't help your credit score by closing accounts or asking that your credit limits be lower. These actions can hurt your score.

- ◆ Checking your credit report will not hurt your credit score as long as you request the report and don't ask a friend at the bank to do it for you.

- ◆ Shopping around for the best interest rates won't hurt your score as long as you do it over a short period of time.

- ◆ Putting a statement in your file won't impact your credit score at all—either for the good or the bad.

- ◆ Bankruptcy is the worst thing you can do for your credit score, but it doesn't mean that you won't ever be able to get credit again.

Part 2

Maintaining Your Score

Some basic good financial habits can help you get and maintain a top credit score. In this part, I talk about how to establish a credit score and work toward keeping it as high as possible. I also explore how your credit score can impact your insurance rates and how to improve your score before applying for a major loan.

Chapter 6

Setting Up Your Score

In This Chapter

- ◆ Opening bank accounts
- ◆ Establishing credit
- ◆ Getting a loan
- ◆ Having a creditless score

You'll find it hard to get credit if you don't have a credit score. So how do you find out if you have one and what do you do if you don't?

In this chapter, I talk about how to find out whether you have a credit score and then how to go about building one if you don't.

Checking to Be Sure You Have a Credit Score

Have you ever tried to apply for a credit card and were told that you've been denied because you don't have a credit history? It's probably because you haven't used credit in the past or just haven't used it enough.

The first thing you should do if you find yourself in this situation is to order your credit score. MyFICO is the best place to get a score for all three of the key credit reporting agencies. You can order your credit scores online at www.myfico.com.

When you get the report, you'll find out whether you have a score and you'll get suggestions for how to improve your score. If you don't have a credit history, the report will probably indicate that you need to establish credit accounts and a good payment history to improve your score.

Credit scores can't be built overnight. It will take several years to get your score in good shape, if you haven't used credit before. But I'll give you some ideas about how to get one established as quickly and painlessly as possible.

Be aware that you must be 18 years old to apply for credit alone in your name. Some people put their younger children on as an authorized user before the age of 18. If you are an authorized user on a card the credit history for that card sometimes will be combined with yours. It's good practice for using credit responsibly, while also having the support of a parent to learn how to do it responsibly.

Establishing Checking and Savings Accounts

If you don't have a checking and savings account set up, do so right away. Although these don't show up on your credit report, they do give creditors the idea that you are financially stable and responsible.

In addition, by setting up a checking and savings account you will establish a working relationship with a bank, which may ultimately be one of the first financial institutions to give you a credit card.

One of the first pieces of plastic you'll get in your own name will be a debit card. These cards can be used at ATMs (automatic teller machines) to get cash. Most banks also give these cards a VISA or MasterCard logo so you can use them as credit cards. Be careful though; the amount that you charge using the debit card is taken directly out of your checking account. Although it looks like a credit card, it doesn't work like one.

If you plan to work with a debit card, be sure you understand how to challenge a charge you did not authorize and how quickly the money will be replaced in your account. I certainly recommend that you keep most of your cash in a savings account not attached to the debit card and only keep a small portion of your cash in the checking account that is attached to the debit card. That way, most of your money will be safe even if your debit card is lost or stolen. The fraudulent user will only be able to use the card for the small amount of money you have in the checking account. While you're waiting for the challenge of the fraudulent charges to be completed, you can use the money in your savings account to open a new checking account. You definitely want to close the account that was used fraudulently.

> **Credit Cautions**
>
> Be aware that the danger of using debit cards is that if they are lost or stolen, fraudulent charges come directly out of your checking account. Even though you can challenge it and get the money back, it can take 30 to 60 days, depending on your bank.

Getting Your First Credit

A good time to get your first credit card is when you are still a college student. Creditors are much more lenient about approving credit for college students. But don't go crazy and get a bunch of cards. Although you probably can get them, you also can get yourself in a deep credit mess and destroy your credit history even before you get a chance to establish a good one.

Credit card companies don't worry about college students because they expect that their parents will help them out of a mess if they get into one. So take advantage of the fact that you can get credit while in college and start to establish your own credit history. If you don't and you try to get your first card after college you will find it harder to get approval for that first credit card.

If you don't plan to go to college, you will have more of a challenge getting your first card. Usually you'll find it easier to get a credit card with a gas company, such as Shell or Exxon, or at a retail store, such as

Wal-Mart or Target. After you've established a good payment history with those cards, you will then find it easier to successfully apply for VISA or MasterCard.

When everything else fails, you can always start with a secured credit card. With this type of card, you will need to deposit a certain amount in a savings account that is equal to the amount of credit you are given—essentially you are securing the credit with your own cash.

You may wonder why that's a good idea. Well by starting with a secure credit card it gives you the opportunity to establish a history and show that you can use credit responsibly and pay your bills on time.

In about 6 to 12 months, you'll probably be able to apply for an unsecured credit card. When you do, you can cancel the secured credit card. You may even be able to find a secured credit card that converts to a regular, unsecured card in a year or so. Just be sure to compare the terms for the converted secured card with those you can get by applying for an unsecured credit card. You certainly don't want to keep the converted secured credit card if you can get better terms applying for a new unsecured credit card.

> **Scoring Tips**
>
> You can compare secured credit card offers at Bankrate.com. Your best offers will include cards that don't have application fees, have low annual fees, and allow you to convert to a regular credit card in about a year.

Using Someone Else's Good Name

You can speed up the process of establishing credit by using someone else's good credit history, but be sure they have a good credit history before you ask for the favor. For example, you can ask your parent or other relative to add you to their credit card as a joint user. Usually the credit reporting agencies will pick this up and add the other's credit history to yours.

Another way to get credit is to ask a parent or relative to cosign a loan with you. That can help you get your first installment loan. Your cosigner will have to be a very close friend or relative because if you don't pay the bill, they will have to pay it. Your cosigner's credit history could be destroyed if you don't live up to your credit obligations.

Be careful though; using someone else's good name to get credit is taking on a major responsibility to that person. If you don't live up to your credit obligations, it's a good way to not only destroy that person's credit history, but also destroy a friendship or family relationship.

Taking Installment Loans

After you've shown that you can be responsible with using credit cards for 6 to 12 months, it's time to apply for your first installment loan. An installment loan can be a small personal loan taken out with your bank or a car loan. Now you won't be able to apply for a new expensive Cadillac, but you should be able to get a small loan for a used car.

You credit score will take a nice boost after you get your first install-ment loan established and show that you make your payments on time. You credit score will be higher if you have a mix of revolving accounts (credit cards) and installment loans (car loans and personal loans).

Can You Get a Credit Score Without Credit?

Although it can be difficult to get a credit score without a credit card, Fair Isaac does have a FICO for you called the Expansion Score. To collect information for this score, Fair Isaac collects information from nontraditional sources of information including the following:

◆ Payday lenders

◆ Check monitoring companies—Stores that run your checks through a machine to see if they are good. The machine is often connected to a check monitoring company that will alert the retailer if you bounce checks frequently.

◆ Rent-to-own stores, such as Aaron's or Enterprise—You pay a monthly amount to rent furniture or electronics with the possi-bility of owning the items in the future.

◆ Utility information—Your past billing history from utility companies.

◆ Public records—Court judgments, liens, and so forth.

The Expansion Score is relatively new and not tested in the marketplace, so it is unknown whether creditors will accept its validity. But even with this score a creditor can quickly see whether you pay your bills on time and handle a checking account responsibly. If you tend to bounce checks, that will also be picked up with this score.

Getting your first credit card can be difficult, especially if you are not a college student, but don't hesitate to start with a small secured credit card, even if it only has a $200 to $500 credit limit.

A secure credit card of any size will give you the opportunity to show that you can handle credit wisely and that you will pay your bills on time. Maintaining a good credit history with even a small credit limit will go a long way to establishing a credit score. Within a year or two you'll be able to get traditional unsecured credit cards with reasonable credit limits as long as you show that you can be a responsible credit user.

The Least You Need to Know

- ◆ Open a checking and savings account to begin establishing a credit history. Although this won't show up on a credit report it gives you an opportunity to establish a banking relationship and shows that you can manage your money responsibly.

- ◆ If you're in college, you'll probably be able to get a traditional unsecured credit card. If not you'll likely have to start with a secured credit card.

- ◆ You can jumpstart your credit history by using a friend or family member's good name, but do so cautiously. You can ruin a friendship or family relationship if you're not responsible with the credit.

- ◆ You can get a credit score without credit called the FICO Expansion Score, but it is relatively new to the market and its acceptance by lenders is still unknown.

Chapter 7

Paying Your Bills On Time

In This Chapter

- ◆ Learning key reasons for timeliness
- ◆ Determining scoring disasters
- ◆ Getting some timely tips

You may think it's an easy task to get your bills paid on time, but many people seem to have great difficulty doing just that. In fact, a missed payment is the most common problem seen on most credit reports.

You can blame it on the mail or on the fact that you forgot to sign a check, but for whatever reason, if you're more than 30 days late, a negative mark is placed on your credit report and it could result in higher interest rates on all your credit cards. In this chapter, I talk about why a late payment can be so devastating to your credit history and how you can avoid getting caught in this trap.

Why It's Important to Pay On Time

Your payment history makes up one third of your credit score, so any negative mark against that history will have a major impact. Creditors look for any sign that you may be heading toward trouble paying your bills. A late payment is seen as the first sign of trouble, and you pay dearly for that sign.

In fact, you can face higher interest rates with all your creditors and even higher insurance premiums when you're late on only one of your cards because your credit score will go down. Many credit cards have a clause in their agreement called the universal default clause, which states that if you pay any bills late, even to other creditors, your interest rate may be increased even if you pay a particular credit card bill on time. That means if you're late with just one lender, and all your other lenders put the universal default clause in their credit agreement, you can end up with higher rates on all the cards with agreement.

As you get into the practice of monitoring your credit report, you will find that your current lenders periodically check your credit report even if you haven't asked for an increase in your credit limit. That's because they are checking to be sure you are keeping up on all your credit obligations. If they see late payments, they become concerned that you are overextended and may be more of a credit risk than originally anticipated. The universal default clause gives them the right to increase your interest rate if they see signs that you may be a higher credit risk even though you haven't missed a payment.

People have seen their credit card interest rates jump from 12 percent to more than 30 percent just because they have a couple of late payments on other cards. Some people even report that the universal default clause was imposed just because they forgot to pay for a $25 book club bill or missed a phone bill.

Credit card interest rates are set on a state by state basis. States that have either weak or no *usury laws* attract most of the major credit card companies. These states include Arizona (Bank of America and Direct Merchants), Delaware (JP Morgan Chase, MBNA, Morgan Stanley [Discover], and HSBC), New Hampshire (Providian), South Dakota (Citibank), Utah (American Express), and Virginia (Capital One). If you have a credit card with any one of these banks, it's likely that your credit card agreement includes a universal default clause and that your interest rates can rise dramatically.

On June 22, 2006, New York became the first state to outlaw the universal default clause, so if you live in New York you are immune to this penalty. Hopefully other states will follow suit.

def•i•ni•tion

Usury laws protect the public from the charging of unreasonable or relatively high interest rates. The word comes from the Medieval Latin word *usuria*, which means "interest" or "excessive interest."

What should you do if you find your interest rates have shot up because of a late payment? Pay off that card as quickly as you can and close the account. Find another credit card that does not have a universal default clause. Unfortunately, that can be difficult to do if you have a poor payment history. If you have many cards that have shot up to near 30 percent interest, it's time to work with a credit counselor who may be able to negotiate lower rates for you. I talk more about how those work in Chapter 13.

What Happens to Your Score When You're Late

Whenever a creditor reports to the credit reporting agencies that you made a late payment, your credit score goes down. Creditors do not report you as late if you are only a few days late. Most creditors will not report you as late until you are more than 30 days late. But there is no reason to take the risk; just pay your bills on time.

If you have a spotless payment history and credit score and you miss a payment, your score could go down almost 100 points. That's because creditors believe that when you have a late payment it is a sign that you are in financial distress and will likely have more trouble paying your bills.

Believe it or not, when I ran the FICO simulator on missing all payments versus missing just one payment in a month I found very little difference. The score for a person with a 750 FICO score (near a perfect score of 850) would go down between 55 and 105 points. That same person would lose between 65 and 125 for missing all payments. After your score goes down it can take months, or even years, of on-time payments to regain your previous high score.

I only found two scenarios that would drop your credit score by more points than a missed payment—maxing out all your credit cards (score would drop by 90 to 140 points) and declaring bankruptcy (score would drop by 205 to 265 points).

You can see from these impacts on your score that the FICO score is heavily weighted to be sure you pay your bills on time. The score is weighted to look for signs that you may be heading into a situation where you won't be able to pay your bills.

The most positive thing you can do to regain your previous high credit score is to pay down 90 to 100 percent of all your credit card balances. In other words, get yourself to a debt utilization ratio of 10 percent or less. For example, if you are currently carrying a total debt load of $2,000 on credit cards with a total credit limit of $4,000 on those cards, your debt utilization ratio is 50 percent. If you pay that debt down to $400, your debt utilization ratio would be 10 percent and you will have paid off 90 percent of your available credit.

Paying down your bills by 90 to 100 percent of your credit card balances can result in an increase of your credit score by 40 to 78 points. Although it may not get you all the way back to your previous high score, if you lost 100 points for a late payment it will get you close. Continued on-time payments will eventually get you back to where you were.

Discovering Tips for Being On Time

What can you do to avoid those late payments? Luckily with automatic bill payment, recurring credit charges, online bill payment, and electronic reminders, it couldn't be easier today for you to pay your bills on time.

Keep in mind that even if you don't receive a bill, it's still due. You can't use the excuse that the bill got lost in the mail to avoid late fees and interest charges—and ultimately a black mark on your credit report. Keep a list of all your bills and their due dates and check off when they're paid each month.

Automatic Payment

If there is a bill that you have a tendency to forget about or that arrives so close to the due date you almost always end up with a late fee, consider setting up an automatic payment plan, if that is an available option. With this type of plan you sign an agreement to allow the creditor to automatically deduct the payment from your checking account when it is due.

Don't worry about giving someone access to your account. Federal law prohibits vendors from taking out more than you authorize. If the vendor makes a mistake they must replace any money they took in error. Errors in automatic payments are a relatively rare occurrence, but they do happen.

Utility companies, who tend to send the bill very close to the due date, are among the best candidates for this type of payment. Often if there is any delay with the mail, the bill from the utility company can show up in your mailbox just one or two days before the bill is due.

Utility companies, especially telephone companies, also tend to be the first ones to report a late bill and they won't hesitate to send you to collections for nonpayment relatively quickly. You can avoid even the possibility of this happening by setting up an automatic payment.

Scoring Tips

Some people get in trouble with the automatic payment method because they don't have enough cash in the bank and they forgot a payment was due. If you choose this method be sure to keep a "pad" of extra cash in your account. You also can avoid a problem by setting up an electronic alert several days prior to the date the automatic payment will be withdrawn. I talk about various electronic alert methods in the sections that follow.

Some companies will even give you a discount if you agree to an automatic payment plan. The biggest problem you may have with this method is that an automatic payment attempt could be made when you don't have enough cash in the account because you forgot about the payment.

Recurring Credit Card Charge

If you have a monthly bill that you must pay each month but tend to forget about, you may want to consider a recurring credit card charge. That way the bill is paid automatically using your credit card.

I don't recommend that you use this solution often because it increases your credit card balances unless you pay them in full each month. But sometimes you can get a discount if you authorize a recurring credit card charge rather than require that a vendor, such as your health or auto insurance company, bill you directly. In fact some insurance companies require that you either accept a recurring credit card charge or an automatic payment plan if you want to pay monthly. Without agreeing to one of those options, you will likely be billed quarterly, semiannually, or annually, which means you must pay a much larger chunk at one time.

You should only consider the recurring credit card option if you pay your credit cards in full each month. Also, this works best with only very small monthly billing amounts to be sure you won't end up paying interest on a basic monthly charge.

Online Bill Payment

My favorite method of bill payment, to be sure I pay everything on time and maintain control of when and how much is paid, is to use online bill payment. I know that some people warn against online bill payment, but as long as you are working with a reputable bank, I don't expect you'll have much of a problem. Many banks offer free online bill payment. If yours doesn't, find one that does before you choose this bill payment option.

Online bill payment has been around for many years and I haven't heard any recent stories of a problem with the systems. The banks have encoded them very well and as long as you carefully protect your access passwords, as well as change them periodically, you should find this a safe alternative.

I prefer this method of payment because you maintain better control of the payment. If you have a dispute with a creditor, you can adjust the payment accordingly in a matter of seconds. That's not as easy to do if you authorize automatic bill payment or a recurring credit charge.

I do this even for bills that do not have the same payment amount each month. That way it serves as a reminder that a bill is due. You have to pick a monthly payment amount to set this up, but the amount can be changed when the bill comes in.

If for some reason I don't get the bill before it's time to pay, I can also find the information on the creditor's website or call for the amount of payment due. That way if a bill gets lost in the mail, I don't risk forgetting to

Scoring Tips

If you do use an online bill payment service, be sure to stay alert for address or account number changes. Every few months, double check the billing address you include in the account information with your online bill payer to be sure your bank has the correct information about your creditors. If your bank sends a payment to the wrong address, it can arrive late, and you can end up having to pay late charges.

make a payment. The worst that can happen is that the automatic payment amount I set up is sent on time and I may still owe a bit more or end up with a credit toward a future billing. Either way I don't risk a late payment.

When I receive a bill in the mail, I verify that the payment is set up for the correct amount and on the correct date. Many of my bills can be paid electronically, which allows the payment to be made closer to the due date or even on the due date.

If you don't have access to online banking, you can still pay online with many creditors. Many credit card and utility companies allow you to pay online using their secure websites. But be sure a website is secure before giving any information regarding your bank account. Always type in the URL you know to be correct for the company you want to pay. Don't just click on a link in an e-mail. Sometimes those e-mails may look like they came from your bank or creditor, but they really didn't. I talk more about that in Chapters 16 and 17.

Remind Yourself Electronically

If you're not comfortable with using any of these bill paying methods, you may find an electronic reminder works better for you. You can remind yourself electronically in the following ways.

◆ Setting up an alert on your Blackberry or other personal data assistant.

◆ Finding out if your Internet service provider offers you an e-mail reminder service.

◆ Using the bill-reminder features if you have personal finance software, such as Quicken or Money.

◆ Setting up e-mail reminders from your creditors, if they offer the service.

◆ Using the calendar feature of your e-mail program to give you alerts. You can set up an appointment for paying your bills and set up to be automatically reminded prior to that appointment. For example, if your Citicorp credit card bill is due on the fifteenth of the month, set up a monthly appointment reminder on your calendar with an alert one week prior to the due date. That way you'll never forget that the bill is due, even if you don't get the bill in the mail.

Pay Bills As Soon As You Get Them

If you're not comfortable with any of these automatic options and prefer to do things the old-fashioned way, then get into the habit of paying your bills as soon as you get them. Each night after you open the mail, write out the checks for any bill that is due and put them in the mailbox.

You can never be hurt by paying a bill early, but you can be punished severely for paying even one bill late. Why take the chance?

If you do choose the old-fashioned method, be sure you have a list of all bills due and check off each month when they are paid. That way if a bill gets lost in the mail, you won't forget about it.

Change Your Due Date

Many credit card companies will work with you if a due date for your bill does not fall on a convenient day of the month. For example, suppose you are paid twice a month and the first check goes primarily to pay the mortgage and other household expenses. The second check is used to pay other creditors.

In this scenario, it's much easier for you to have your credit cards due between the fifteenth and thirtieth of the month. Call all your credit card companies and ask them to adjust your due date to one that better matches when you will have the money available to pay. That way, you can ease your financial strain of paying too many bills at one time and ending up paying some bills late. It's all a matter of managing your cash flow and getting your bill due dates closer to when you know you will actually have the cash.

If you just don't have enough cash to pay your bills on time, then you are overextended and the only answer for you is to pay down the debt and stop charging any new debt until you are in a better position financially.

Of course, the best financial position for anyone to be in is to have no debt. If you can get yourself there, go for it. Unfortunately with the housing, transportation, and health-care costs today, few families are able to live completely debt-free.

The Least You Need to Know

- ◆ You can end up with higher interest rates on all your cards if just one of your bills is paid late.

- ◆ One late payment can devastate a good credit score.

- ◆ Take advantage of one of the new methods of payment available today to be sure you pay your bills on time, including automatic bill payment, recurring credit charges, or online bill paying.

8

Reducing Your Debt

In This Chapter

- ◆ Depleting debt
- ◆ Establishing debt strategies
- ◆ Restricting credit
- ◆ Looking for money

If you want to improve your credit score by reducing your debt, your strategies for paying down debt may need to be different than those financial planners and credit counselors tell you about. Although it makes good sense to use a snowball approach to pay off your debt, that approach may not help you increase your credit score.

In this chapter, I review two key strategies for paying down your debt—one for reducing it faster by minimizing interest expenses and one that helps you improve your credit score more quickly. I also give you some ideas on how to find more money to pay down your debt.

Pay Off Your Debt, Don't Just Move It

Have you been playing the game of moving your debt to the lowest interest rate credit cards you can find—maybe even as low as 0 percent for six months or a year? Although it's great to take advantage of those low rates, you also must use the time you get at the low rate to pay off your balances. Too many people are just jumping from card to card while they continue to increase their debt levels. Why not—especially if you can keep finding those 0 percent cards?

Well if you're concerned about your credit score, and you should be if you want to keep getting low interest rate credit offers, stop doing it and pay off your debt. Applying for more and more credit cards and then transferring your balances is gradually reducing your credit score. Each time you get a new card your credit score goes down a bit, maybe only 10 to 20 points, but if you get new cards often enough you could get yourself into credit score trouble and find it harder and harder to get those great credit offers.

You should have a strategy for paying down debt, not just moving it around. There are two good strategies—round robin and snowball effect. If getting your credit score up to the highest number is your priority because you plan to buy a house and need a good credit score to get the best mortgage offer, then the round robin strategy is best for you. With this strategy you'll pay off all your balances on all your cards down to the lowest possible percentage of your credit limit. For example, you should try to get all your cards down to no more than 10 percent of your credit limit. That alone could increase your score by 30 to 70 points.

If getting rid of that debt is most important, then use the snowball effect, which is paying down your highest credit card first and then using the extra cash to pay down the next highest card. I discuss how to implement each strategy in this chapter.

Developing Strategies for Paying Down Your Debt

No matter which strategy you choose, you must decide to pay down your debt and stop charging. Let's take a look at how both the snowball effect and round robin strategy help you pay down that debt.

Pushing a Snowball Downhill

Every financial planner you talk with will put you on a plan to pay off your debt as quickly as possible. That makes good sense and it should definitely be your goal no matter what you hope to do when the debt is gone.

Many financial planners will talk about a pay-down strategy called the *snowball effect*. For this payoff strategy, you use any excess cash you have to pay down the highest interest rate credit card first, while paying only the minimum balance on your other cards. That way you minimize the amount of interest you must pay.

Think of the snowball effect as slowly building up the size of your snowball then getting the snowball moving faster and faster by pushing it downhill. To use the strategy you start by paying off your highest interest credit card

def•i•ni•tion

The **snowball effect** uses the strategy of paying off debt by paying off your highest interest rate cards first, which makes a lot of sense from a financial planning perspective because you reduce your interest expenses. But this strategy may not help you increase your credit score. If increasing your credit score is a priority, then reducing your balance to about 30 percent of your credit limit on all your credit cards is more important. That's done using the round robin strategy.

first. Each time you pay off a card you add what you were currently paying on the highest interest credit card to the minimum balance of the next highest interest rate card until all your credit cards are paid off. Then use the large lump of cash you were using to pay down credits to pay off installment loans. When those are paid off you can then use the large lump to pay off your mortgage more quickly.

For example, suppose you have three credit cards that you've maxed out. Credit card A with 18 percent interest has a balance of $1,000 (minimum payment $15), credit card B with 15 percent interest has a balance of $2,000 (minimum payment $20), and credit card C with 12 percent interest has a balance of $3,000 (minimum payment $35). In addition, you have a car loan with 6 percent interest and a balance of $10,000 (minimum payment of $150 per month). Finally you have a mortgage with a payment of $1,000 per month.

Now let's look at how the snowball effect works. Suppose you have a total of $1,500 per month to pay your bills and you pay them down using the snowball effect. To keep this simple, I'm not going to calculate interest each month. Interest charges will, of course, slow down the snowball effect because balances will not go down as quickly.

Month 1 you would use the $1,500 to pay:

Credit Card A	$295
Credit Card B	$20
Credit Card C	$35
Car Loan	$150
Mortgage	$1,000

Remaining balances (not considering interest) would be:

Credit Card A	$1,000 – $295 = $705
Credit Card B	$2,000 – $20 = $1,980
Credit Card C	$3,000 – $35 = $2,965
Car Loan	$10,000 – $150 = $9,850

Month 2 you would use the $1,500 to pay:

Credit Card A	$295
Credit Card B	$20
Credit Card C	$35
Car Loan	$150
Mortgage	$1,000

Remaining balances (not considering interest) would be:

Credit Card A	$705 – $295 = $410
Credit Card B	$1,980 – $20 = $1,960
Credit Card C	$2,965 – $35 = $2,930
Car Loan	$9,850 – $150 = $9,700

Month 3 you would use the $1,500 to pay:

Credit Card A	$295
Credit Card B	$20
Credit Card C	$35
Car Loan	$150
Mortgage	$1,000

Remaining balances (not considering interest) would be:

Credit Card A	$410 – $295 = $115
Credit Card B	$1,960 – $20 = $1,940
Credit Card C	$2,930 – $35 = $2,895
Car Loan	$9,700 – $150 = $9,550

Month 4 you would use the $1,500 to pay:

Credit Card A	$115
Credit Card B	$200
Credit Card C	$35
Car Loan	$150
Mortgage	$1,000

Remaining balances (not considering interest) would be:

Credit Card A	$115 – $115 = $0
Credit Card B	$1,940 – $200 = $1,740
Credit Card C	$2,895 – $35 = $2,860
Car Loan	$9,550 – $150 = $9,400

You can see that in four months, credit card A is paid off and you can put the extra money toward credit card B. The extra money with credit card A paid off will increase from $295 to $315 ($295 toward credit card B plus the $20 you were paying to credit card B).

In about six additional months when credit card B is paid off, all the extra money can go toward paying off credit card C. So you can then start paying credit card C $350 ($315 plus $35 you were paying toward credit card C). In about 13 additional months you would then have credit card C paid off and can get started on paying the car loan faster.

When credit card C is paid off you can then pay $500 toward your car loan ($350 from paying off credit card C plus $150 of what you were already paying on the car loan). Finally when the car loan is paid off you can then pay $1,500 toward your mortgage ($500 from the car loan plus $1,000 you were already paying).

You can see from this example that the amount you'll be able to use to pay down debt is like a snowball that gradually grows in size as it continues to move downhill. You start with just $295 extra to pay your bills and in about two years you have $350 extra to pay toward your car. When that's paid off you'll have $500 extra per month to pay toward your mortgage or to save toward a new car.

Round Robin Payoff Strategy

Although the snowball effect is a great strategy to minimize interest payments because you get rid of your highest interest cards first and then have more money to pay toward principal, this strategy won't help your credit score much because you will still be carrying nearly maximum balances on your other credit cards until they are all paid off. In this scenario it would probably be about a three-year period to pay off all the cards because interest charges would accrue on the unpaid balances, which I did not include in the calculations to keep things simple.

If improving your credit score is critical, you should use a round robin strategy to pay down debt. With this strategy you concentrate on paying down all your debt to about 30 percent of the credit limit on each card. When all three cards are paid down to 30 percent, then you concentrate on getting them down to 20 percent and finally down to 10 percent. When you reach the 10 percent goal, your credit score should be up by at least 30 points and possibly as much as 70 points. If you've had a history of late payments and start paying all your cards on time, that alone could increase your credit score by as much as 40 points.

If you want your credit score to improve more quickly, then a round robin strategy would work better for you, but you will end up paying more interest and it will take longer to pay off your debt completely. Let's use the same scenario that we just discussed to see how the round robin strategy works. Remember I said that all the cards had been maxed out. That means credit card A has a credit limit of $1,000, credit card B has a credit limit of $2,000, and credit card C has a credit limit of $3,000.

Month 1 you would use the $1,500 to pay:

Credit Card A	$295
Credit Card B	$20
Credit Card C	$35
Car Loan	$150
Mortgage	$1,000

Remaining balances (not considering interest) would be:

Credit Card A	$1,000 – $295 = $705
Credit Card B	$2,000 – $20 = $1,980
Credit Card C	$3,000 – $35 = $2,965
Car Loan	$10,000 – $150 = $9,850

Month 2 you would use the $1,500 to pay:

Credit Card A	$295
Credit Card B	$20
Credit Card C	$35
Car Loan	$150
Mortgage	$1,000

Remaining balances (not considering interest) would be:

Credit Card A	$705 – $295 = $410
Credit Card B	$1,980 – $20 = $1,960
Credit Card C	$2,965 – $35 = $2,930
Car Loan	$9,850 – $150 = $9,700

Month 3 you would use the $1,500 to pay:

Credit Card A	$110
Credit Card B	$205
Credit Card C	$35
Car Loan	$150
Mortgage	$1,000

Remaining balances (not considering interest) would be:

Credit Card A	$410 – $110 = $300
Credit Card B	$1,960 – $205 = $1,735
Credit Card C	$2,930 – $35 = $2,895
Car Loan	$9,700 – $150 = $9,550

Note that when using the round robin strategy you start paying down credit card B more quickly in month 3 because credit card A is now 30 percent of its credit limit ($300 of $3,000). Now you will pay only the minimum balance on credit card A, which is $10.

Month 4 you would use the $1,500 to pay:

Credit Card A	$10
Credit Card B	$305
Credit Card C	$35
Car Loan	$150
Mortgage	$1,000

Remaining balances (not considering interest) would be:

Credit Card A	$300 – 10 = $290
Credit Card B	$1,735 – $305 = $1,430
Credit Card C	$2,895 – $35 = $2,860
Car Loan	$9,550 – $150 = $9,400

Month 5 you would use the $1,500 to pay:

Credit Card A	$10
Credit Card B	$305
Credit Card C	$35
Car Loan	$150
Mortgage	$1,000

Remaining balances (not considering interest) would be:

Credit Card A	$290 – $10 = $280
Credit Card B	$1,430 – $305 = $1,125
Credit Card C	$2,860 – $35 = $2,825
Car Loan	$9,400 – $150 = $9,250

Month 6 you would use the $1,500 to pay:

Credit Card A	$10
Credit Card B	$305
Credit Card C	$35
Car Loan	$150
Mortgage	$1,000

Remaining balances (not considering interest) would be:

Credit Card A	$280 – $10 = $270
Credit Card B	$1,125 – $305 = $820
Credit Card C	$2,825 – $35 = $2,790
Car Loan	$9,250 – $150 = $9,100

Month 7 you would use the $1,500 to pay:

Credit Card A	$10
Credit Card B	$220
Credit Card C	$255
Car Loan	$150
Mortgage	$1,000

Remaining balances (not considering interest) would be:

Credit Card A	$270 – $10 = $260
Credit Card B	$820 – $220 = $600
Credit Card C	$2,790 – $255 = $2,535
Car Loan	$9,100 – $150 = $8,950

You can see by month 7 you now use only 30 percent of the available credit limit for credit cards A and B and you can move on to paying down credit card C more quickly until you get that one down to 30 percent. Beginning in month 8 you would be able to pay down credit card C by $320 with $10 going to credit card A, $20 going to credit card B, $150 for the car loan, and $1,000 for the mortgage. With that much going to credit card C you can get it paid down to $900 (30 percent of its $3,000 credit limit) in about five to six months.

Credit Cautions _____

Whatever strategy you choose you will need to limit how much you charge. If you continue to charge, it will take that much longer to get your balances down to meet your debt-paying goals.

By using the round robin strategy all your cards could be down to the goal of 30 percent of your available credit limits in about 13 months and you'll see a nice jump in your credit score, possibly as much as 30 to 50 points. Using the snowball effect strategy could take as long as two to three years with this scenario to get that impact because you'd carry cards to the max that much longer.

Limiting How Much You Charge

During your payoff period, if you are trying to improve your credit score, don't even think of getting another card. Even if you get a card and pay it off each month to take care of the other spending you do, it could still have a negative impact on your credit score.

The FICO score is based on the balance reported by the credit card companies; it doesn't look at how much you're paying each month. So if you charge $1,000 per month on a card that has a maximum limit of $1,200 per month, it will look as though you are nearly maxing out that card even if you pay off that amount in full the next month.

Finding Money for Debt Payoff

Now the big question you may have is how do you find that extra cash so you can put one of these two payoff strategies into action? I recommend to people that they take the time during a month to write down every penny they spend. Yes, I know that's a real pain to do, but you'll be amazed at how much you learn about yourself and your spending patterns by doing this.

At the end of the month, rank each of your expenditures with a number from 1 to 5. Give the number 1 to expenses that must be incurred no matter what—your mortgage and other debt payments—as well as any savings you definitely want to do. Give the number 2 to important items but not required items. Give number 5 to things you could have skipped completely. Give the number 4 to things you probably could have skipped, but wanted anyway. Give the number 3 to items that you wanted but could have been put off a month.

Now add up all your 1s, 2s, 3s, 4s, and 5s. Suppose you came out with a calculation such as this:

$1,700: Total of 1s

$600: Total of 2s

$400: Total of 3s

$200: Total of 4s

$100: Total of 5s

Now suppose you decide you want to make paying down debt a priority and you can skip all the number 4s and 5s or at least limit them to $50 and cut down some of the 3s to get yourself an extra $300 per month for paying down debt.

You've got your snowball or the start of the cash you need to begin the round robin. If getting your debt paid off is the priority, then get your snowball rolling. If you want to improve your credit score first, then begin your round robin.

The Least You Need to Know

◆ Paying off your debt, not just moving it around to find the best interest rate while it continues to build, must be your priority if you want to improve your credit score.

◆ If paying off debt is your priority, try the snowball effect.

◆ If improving your credit score is your priority, then start jumping around with your debt payoff similar to a robin.

Chapter 9

Staying Credit Worthy

In This Chapter

- ◆ Keeping credit balances low
- ◆ Having emergency funds
- ◆ Getting insured
- ◆ Avoiding divorce disaster

Almost as important as your name is your credit worthiness. Without a good credit score, your ability to do what you want, when you want to do it, will be hampered by your financial reputation.

You'll have a more difficult time getting credit for the things you want to do or you'll pay a lot more to get that credit. You could end up with higher insurance premiums and you may even find it difficult to get some jobs with a poor credit history.

In this chapter, I focus on how to keep yourself credit worthy and get the best credit rates, the lowest insurance premiums, and a good financial history in case a potential employer checks it.

Paying Off Balances

By far, the best thing you can do to maintain your highest credit score is to pay off your credit balances. Now I don't mean that you'll get the best score by paying balances in full every month. I mean you get your best score by not carrying more than 10 percent of your total allowable credit on any one card.

Even if you do pay your balances in full, that payoff might happen after your credit card company has already reported the higher level of credit use to the credit reporting agencies. For example, suppose you charge $1,500 on a credit card with a credit limit of $2,000. That means you used 75 percent of your available credit.

Now suppose that your credit statement is sent on November 1 and reported to the credit reporting agencies on that date. You pay off your balance on November 5 and start charging again up to a level of about $1,200. That means you used 60 percent of your available credit. When the statement is sent on December 1 and reported to the credit reporting agencies, it will look like you paid only $300 and are still carrying a large balance.

The FICO score does not calculate how much you pay toward your credit card balance each month and has no way to know that in actuality you pay off your credit cards each month. If you pay off your balances each month and want to improve your credit score, you need to make sure those payoffs reach your credit card company before it sends the report to the credit reporting agencies in order to get and keep a high credit score.

Here are other things you can do to keep your credit score high by paying off balances:

- If you start paying your bills on time every month and you weren't doing so before, that can raise your credit score by 30 points in about a year.

- If you stop charging and pay a significant amount toward your existing credit, you could raise your credit score as much as 40 points in six months.

- If you pay off all your credit cards to zero, then that could raise your credit score 10 to 75 points, depending on how high your credit score was before your payoff. A person with a high credit score already won't benefit as much as someone with a mediocre score.

Avoid Maxing Out Your Credit Cards

One of the worst things you can do to your credit worthiness is to max out all your credit cards to their credit limit. That could decrease your credit score by 50 to 100 points. The only thing that would hurt your credit score more is to miss payments on all your credit cards (score would go down by 65 to 125 points) or declare bankruptcy (score would go down by 205 to 265).

Your score will be the hardest hit if you have had a good credit history and all of a sudden show some bad tendencies. For example, suppose you always paid your bills on time and all of a sudden started to pay them all late. Your score will then drop 125 points.

FICO is designed to quickly catch someone who shows signs of starting to get into trouble. Your score drops the most significantly if you've maintained a high credit rating and then all of a sudden start showing signs of credit strain by paying bills late.

Credit Cautions

No doubt, bankruptcy will make your credit score drop like a lead balloon, but even paying one card late when you have otherwise spotless credit can reduce your credit score by 55 to 105 points. The better your credit score the more it will drop with a missed payment.

Here are some other actions that can cause your credit rating to go down:

- Miss one payment on an otherwise spotless payment history— Credit score will drop 55 to 105 points.

- Apply for a new credit card—Credit score could go down 10 points, but your credit also may go up 5 or 10 points if you have a good payment history and don't have many other cards.

- Apply for a car loan or mortgage—Credit score could go down 15 points if you have a lot of other credit, but could go up 5 points if you are just building a credit history.

- Transfer balances to a new card with a lower interest rate—Credit score could go down 35 points if you have a lot of other cards, but could go up 5 points if you don't have a lot of credit.

Saving for Emergencies

One of the best ways to avoid credit emergencies that could make you miss a payment or possibly even find the need to file bankruptcy is to build a savings account for emergencies. Most financial planners will tell you to have a cash savings that can cover your bill payments for at least three months. That way if you do experience a job loss or injury you have some time to recover from the loss and figure out a solution before you get into financial trouble.

The majority of people who end up filing for bankruptcy do so because of job loss or a medical emergency. Obviously a job loss means you won't have money coming in to pay the bills. A medical emergency, especially if you don't have health insurance, can quickly build to $20,000; $100,000; or more. If it also means you can't work, then the crisis can get worse even faster. Even emergency savings won't help you get yourself out of a $100,000 hole, but it may help you buy some time until you can figure out another financial solution.

Scoring Tips

Build yourself an emergency fund using a "pay yourself first" strategy. Don't let your credit score and your financial future be destroyed because of a short-term crisis such as a job loss or medical emergency. Have some cash tucked away for emergencies.

To build that emergency savings, start by "paying yourself first." That means before you do anything else each month, set aside money that you put into an emergency savings account. Many companies even allow you to designate a certain amount that can be taken out of your check and automatically deposited into a savings account.

If that's not possible and you use automatic deposit for your paycheck, ask the bank that accepts that check to put a certain amount into savings each month. That way you pay yourself first and don't even have to think about it.

Anyone who is self-employed should think about building an emergency fund that will cover about six months of his bills because his financial situation is more precarious. Most people who are self-employed find themselves in a cash crunch as they wait for payment on work completed, so cash flow can be a problem. You can avoid hurting your credit reputation by having the cash in an emergency fund to pay bills and not risk the penalty of paying late.

Maintaining Adequate Insurance

Being sure you have the right amount of insurance to cover any emergencies can go a long way toward avoiding a credit crisis. Insuring yourself and your key assets is important to being able to recover quickly from a loss.

For example, if you use your car for work and you are in a major car accident where your car is totaled, insurance will cover some of that loss and give you the cash you need to get a replacement vehicle. If you get sick and need surgery, health insurance will pay a large share of that cost and reduce the amount you need to pay out of pocket. If your store burns down because of a fire, business insurance will help pay for the lost merchandise as well as the expenses for rebuilding the store.

Insurance plays two roles—helping you recover more quickly from a loss and minimizing the cash you need to spend out of pocket to recover from that loss. You can more quickly earn the money you need to pay your monthly bills and avoid incurring late fees, as well as a credit score penalty, by maintaining adequate insurance to cover potential losses.

Protecting Your Credit After Divorce

Divorce ruins more people's credit scores than almost any other life-changing event and it can do so long after the divorce is final. That's because any credit card or other loan that you took jointly can come back to haunt you years after the divorce if you didn't shut down the credit during the divorce.

As long as your name is on the credit card or loan as a cosigner or an authorized user, the account can legally be put on your credit report. If your ex-spouse has a poor credit history with missed payments, repossessions, foreclosures, and even a bankruptcy on his credit history, and your name was on any of the troubled accounts, the mess will show up on your credit report.

Credit Cautions

During the process of getting a divorce, protect yourself and your credit by notifying all lenders and creditors from whom you've gotten joint accounts or cosigned a loan. If you've given your soon-to-be ex-spouse permission as an authorized user be sure to notify the lender that you are getting a divorce and your ex-spouse is no longer authorized to use the account. Without that notice your ex-spouse could continue charging on those accounts and not pay the bills, and then you could end up with a destroyed credit history.

When filing for divorce always be sure that any joint credit accounts are closed and your name is removed. Be sure to send a letter warning any of your creditors that you are divorcing and that you will not be held responsible for any credit incurred on the account after the date on your letter. This letter should serve as a freeze on the account. I include a sample letter for this purpose in Appendix C.

Even if you ask to freeze an account, your ex-spouse can often get that account reopened. The only way to be sure your name won't be on a reopened account is to notify the lender or creditor in writing that you are divorcing and will not be responsible for any new charges. If the lender keeps your name on the account after you've alerted him, you then have a legal right to get that negative mark off your credit report. But be sure to keep a copy of your original notification to the lender. Even better, call the lender about a week or two after the notification is sent to be sure the information made it into your credit with the lender and jot down the date and who you spoke with at the creditor company on your copy of the letter.

To make sure you don't forget to notify any lenders, get a copy of your credit report from all three credit reporting agencies. I talked about how to do that in Chapter 3.

Armed with the information you need about existing accounts, take these steps immediately upon deciding to file for divorce or receiving divorce papers from your spouse:

◆ Make a list of all credit cards or loans that show up on your credit report.

◆ If you think your spouse may be an authorized user on any cards in your name, call the creditor to find out. If so, send a letter letting the creditor know that you are divorcing and ask that your soon-to-be ex-spouse be removed as an authorized user.

◆ If you have any joint revolving credit accounts, let the credit card issuer know that you are divorcing and ask that the account be frozen by a specific date and let that creditor know that you will not be responsible for any charges after that date.

◆ If you have joint installment credit, such as a car loan or other secured loan, the only way you will be able to get your name off that loan is to require your spouse to refinance the loan into his or her name. It doesn't help to state in the divorce decree that your spouse will be responsible for that loan. Your agreement with the lender was made before the divorce and if your spouse doesn't make the payments the lender will come after you.

◆ During the divorce process, even if your spouse will ultimately be responsible for the debt, be sure that all payments are made on time. Even one late payment can hurt your credit score severely. Sometimes you may want to accept responsibility for paying off a credit card in exchange for additional cash as part of the divorce settlement. That way you can make sure outstanding debt is paid on time.

◆ If you have secured debt that just can't be refinanced, such as the family home, set a time limit for how long that debt can stay open before the asset securing the debt must be sold. You may end up having to make payments on a home you don't live in just to keep your credit worthy. Don't ever let your name get removed from the ownership of an asset until your name is no longer on the loan for that asset. For example, if as part of the divorce settlement your spouse gets the house, don't *quit-claim* the deed to your spouse until your name is off the mortgage.

def•i•ni•tion _____

Quit-claim is a deed transfer of the ownership of the property. Essentially if you quit-claim the deed on your house to your spouse, you are giving up your title to that property.

If you're just recovering from a messy divorce and your credit score is a disaster, you'll need to find an experienced mortgage broker if you want to buy a new home and apply for a mortgage. An experienced mortgage broker can help you find a lender that does not sell their mortgages on the open market. These types of lenders usually have more lenient rules and will look at your credit history beyond the FICO score. You may need to pay a higher interest rate to get this type of mortgage, but if you want to buy a new home, that may be your only choice.

Staying credit worthy is the most important thing you can do for your financial future. Getting yourself out of debt and then keeping yourself there is certainly the best goal you can have, but in today's world with the rising costs of housing, health care, and other basic necessities, people find it harder and harder to stay out of debt. So your best solution if you can't operate solely on a cash basis is to keep your credit score high and have access to the lowest possible interest rates.

The Least You Need to Know

◆ Being credit worthy is just as important as your good name if you want to maintain a strong financial position.

◆ Paying down debt is the most effective way to improve your credit score.

◆ Missing just one payment if you have an otherwise perfect credit history can devastate your credit score.

◆ Divorce can destroy your credit worthiness if you don't act to protect it as soon as the divorce is filed.

Chapter 10

Insurance and Your Credit Score

In This Chapter

- ◆ Finding the connection
- ◆ Impacting your rates
- ◆ Cutting your insurance costs

You may not realize that your insurance premium can be set based on your credit history. You're not alone. Polls taken recently show that only one third of U.S. citizens realize that their credit history is used when determining their insurance premiums.

In this chapter, I explore how your credit history became a determining factor in your insurance rates, what credit behavior can raise your rates the most, and what steps you should take to improve your score and lower your rates. I also give you a list of the companies that penalize you the most based on credit behaviors.

Discovering the Connection Between Credit Score and Insurance Score

Fair Isaac, the folks behind the FICO score, decided they wanted to expand their business by looking at ways to assist the insurance industry with scoring. In the 1990s, Fair Isaac worked with several insurers to test their theory that credit scores might be a good predictor of home-owner's and auto insurance claims losses. After comparing the data collected from these insurers with Fair Isaac's credit data, they found some correlations between claims and credit history.

In 2000, a study done by Metropolitan Property and Casualty Insurance solidified the theory. For example, the most quoted aspect of that study found that people with accounts on their credit report dating back 25 to 29 years filed only $60 worth of claims for every $100 of premiums. On the other hand, people with credit accounts as old as one year filed $95 in claims per $100 of premiums during the course of three years.

No one knows exactly what the relationship is or what causes it. A spokesman for the Property Casualty Insurers Association of America told *Consumer Reports* in an August 2006 story about how insurance companies link credit reports to insurance premiums, "People with a pattern of irresponsible financial behavior and poor credit history have a much greater chance of being in an accident or filing a claim."

Although the numbers seem to support the fact that insurance companies believe that line, the conclusion from the key study on the subject—the 2000 Metropolitan study—found the links between responsible financial management and future expected losses "unsupported." More study is definitely needed, and the U.S. Federal Trade Commission was conducting such a study at the time this book was written.

Only three states have banned the use of credit scoring for all insurance—California, Hawaii, and Massachusetts. Maryland banned the use of credit scores for homeowner's policies.

Insurance companies are lobbying hard to be sure no other states join that ban. In fact, insurance companies have succeeded in getting a model law that weakly protects consumers passed in 22 states. Basically that law prohibits counting delinquent medical records in the insurance credit score. The rest of your credit history is fair game.

So if you don't live in one of the states that ban credit scoring for the purpose of calculating your insurance premium, you can be fairly certain that your credit history is a factor in setting your premiums. At this point, the insurance companies are not required to divulge your insurance credit score, but most do admit that one aspect of the underwriting process does include looking at your credit history.

> **Scoring Surprises**
>
> Conning & Co., a research firm based in Hartford, Connecticut, found in a 2001 survey that 92 percent of all insurance companies use credit information when rating or underwriting new policies. As of early 2006, all the top five auto insurance companies used insurance credit scoring.

Exploring Impact on Your Premiums

Right now there are two key credit reporting agencies that provide scoring models and credit histories to insurance companies—Fair Isaac and ChoicePoint. Fair Isaac was founded in 1956. ChoicePoint started in 1997 and says it's the "leading provider of decision-making technology and information that helps reduce fraud and mitigate risk." Basically it provides data to the insurance industry, as well as a credit score analysis that some insurance companies use.

Many insurance companies actually set up their own scoring analysis in-house using their large actuarial staffs that combine the credit data they get from credit reporting agencies with their own claims data to determine insurance premiums. These scoring models must be submitted to state insurance regulators. *Consumer Reports* obtained these scoring models from state regulators in Florida, Michigan, and Texas in 2005 to find out the secrets behind insurance credit scoring. Using information from these three states, *Consumer Reports* exposed the secrets of insurance scoring.

> **Scoring Tips**
>
> You can read the details about *Consumer Reports'* August 2006 insurance credit score study at http://autos.msn.com/advice/CRArt.aspx?contentid=4024123.

Consumer Reports found that insurance credit scoring models emphasize bits of credit data. When you see the list you'll probably wonder what this list has to do with your driving record or homeowner's risks. Each company weighs these bits of information differently to determine your insurance credit score and its impact on your insurance premiums. These bits of information include:

◆ Your payment history

◆ Your credit balances

◆ Your credit limits

◆ How frequently you shop for credit

◆ Types of loans you have

On its website, MetLife gives more details of the types of information it uses from a person's credit history to set insurance premiums:

◆ Public record filings, such as bankruptcy, foreclosure, wage garnishment, civil judgment, or tax lien.

◆ Collection activity (excluding those from medical-related providers or facilitates).

◆ Accounts not in good standing or past due.

◆ Amount of outstanding debt in relation to revolving credit limits.

◆ Length of time credit has been established.

◆ Number of newly opened accounts (car loan, credit card, and so on) in the last 24 months.

◆ Number of applications for loans, credit cards, mortgages, or any other form of credit in the last 24 months.

I tried to find similar detail on the other auto insurance company websites, but the information on their websites was much less detailed, even though they did admit to using credit history when determining premiums. All the companies try to put it in a positive light by saying that with a good credit history the customer can get a discount.

In addition to looking at the type of information used, *Consumer Reports* worked with experts to determine how this information was used to determine premiums. Its study focused on three key users of credit data—Progressive, ChoicePoint, and Fair Isaac—but premium discounts and surcharges were calculated for all the major car insurers. I talk more about what they found regarding premiums in a later section.

The experts found that Progressive penalized you for opening one new credit card in the previous four months. They also penalized you if you carried a balance that was more than 40 percent of your credit limit.

ChoicePoint punishes you for having department store charge cards and auto loans from automaker finance companies. You also get punished if you don't have an oil company credit card. If you buy appliances or furniture using finance-company credit, which is common with those six-month, zero-interest installment loans, your insurance credit score will be damaged as well. You can also be punished if you opened one or more new accounts in the last 24 months. Just don't set up any new accounts in the 24 months before you apply for new insurance to be safe against ChoicePoint's wrath.

Fair Isaac punishes you by lowering your insurance credit score if you have one or more credit inquiries in the last 12 months. You are also punished if have any number but two major credit cards.

As part of its study on insurance credit scores, *Consumer Reports* looked at how the premiums varied for a hypothetical 28-year-old male in Orlando, Florida, who drives a Toyota Camry. The study revealed that his insurance premium could be as low as $782 or as high as $4,755 depending on which insurance company he used and how bad his insurance credit score was.

The company that offers the lowest premium for someone with a good credit score is Progressive (annual premium $782), followed closely by Allstate (annual premium $790). The company with the greatest penalty for a bad credit score is Birmingham Fire (AIG) (annual premium $4,755—143 percent surcharge for a bad credit history) followed by State Farm (annual premium $2,600 or a 108 percent surcharge for bad credit).

If you have a bad credit history but an otherwise good driving record, you probably want to at least get a quote from Progressive and Allstate to see whether you can get better rates. People with bad credit history, even though they are safe drivers, will find that their insurance quotes will vary much more greatly than those who have a good credit history and a good driving history.

surance Costs

rnia, Hawaii, or Massachusetts, you don't have to
h how your insurance credit score will impact your
se, you should take some credit management steps
to get the best premium when you apply for a new insurance policy.

Although there is no law requiring insurance companies to expose their
credit scoring practices, based on what was learned by *Consumer Reports*
there are things you can do to be sure you get the lowest premiums.
Most of the actions you can take are similar to those I discussed in
Chapter 8 on the impact reducing your debt can have and in Chapter 11
on fixing your credit report. But there are two significant differences on
insurance credit scoring that *Consumer Reports* revealed:

◆ Don't apply for a new credit card for 24 months before you start
shopping for a new insurance company. Even though Fair Isaac
only penalizes you for shopping in the past 12 months, you have
no way of knowing whose scoring model is being used. Choice-
Point and Progressive both look back 24 months for new credit
applications.

◆ Don't exceed 40 percent of your allowable credit on any one credit
card for the three months prior to applying for new insurance.

Your insurance company may notify you if a negative credit history
impacted your insurance rating, but don't expect to hear from them.
MetLife was the only company that indicated on its website that it
advises its customers when their credit history was used and will let
them know what in their credit history prevented them from getting
the best premium rate. MetLife also indicates that an adverse action
notice is sent when a person first applies for a new policy, as well as at
the time of annual renewal.

Some insurance companies only look at the credit history for new customers. Others check credit history each year before renewing a policy.
You can figure out whether your insurance company inquired about
you credit history by looking at the inquiries section of your credit
report. Review Chapter 3 for more information about how to read your
credit report.

In reviewing the websites of other insurers, AIG, Allstate, GEICO, Liberty Mutual, Nationwide, Progressive, and State Farm all mention that they use credit history in determining an insurance premium. None of these companies gave any indication that they report the reasons for a negative decision in the way that MetLife does.

The Least You Need to Know

◆ Your credit history can and probably does impact the insurance premiums you pay.

◆ Insurers believe there is a correlation between your credit history and the likelihood that you will file a claim.

◆ Minimize the number of new accounts you apply for in the 24 months before you submit an insurance application.

◆ To get the best rates, keep your credit card balances less than 40 percent of your credit limit.

Chapter 11

Fixing Your Score Before Applying for Credit

In This Chapter

- ◆ Reducing credit debt
- ◆ Limiting use
- ◆ Correcting errors
- ◆ Finding out what won't help

If you want to get the best interest rate offer when you apply for a major loan such as a mortgage, fix your credit score before you apply. Depending on how bad your credit score is, it could take as little as two months to as much as several years, but it will save you a lot of money in the future. You'll also be in much better shape financially to take on that major expense.

In this chapter, I talk about the kinds of things you can do to boost your credit score quickly and the types of things that probably won't help.

Tips for Boosting Your Credit Score Quickly

Can you boost your score quickly? Yes, but it may be painful. You need to stop spending on anything but the absolute essentials and instead use all your extra cash to pay down debt. Anything you buy should be bought with cash and not credit. As you pay down your debt, look at your credit reports and correct any mistakes you may find.

Pay Off Credit Cards and Lines of Credit

No doubt, the number-one thing you can do to give your credit score a swift boost is to pay off all your credit cards and lines of credit. If your credit reports show that at least 90 percent of all your credit cards are paid off—that means not more than 10 percent of any credit line is in use—then your credit score could go up as much as 70 points, according to the FICO simulator at myFICO.com.

Credit Cautions

Don't take out another loan to pay off credit cards. If you just don't have the cash, you'll have to find ways to cut spending. In Chapter 8, I talked about strategies for paying down debt. You may be able to borrow from friends or family members for a short time to reduce your credit card balances.

That may not sound like much to you, but if you can increase a FICO score of 650 to 720 your interest rate on a 30-year mortgage could drop by almost 2 percent. Your monthly payment on a $170,000 mortgage could be $200 less per month. In Chapter 1, I talked about the relationship between credit score and interest rates and give you charts that show how much you can save with a higher credit score.

Use Credit Cards Sparingly

While you're trying to boost your credit score, don't use your credit cards unless you are facing a dire emergency. The less you use your cards, the higher your credit score will go.

As you pay down your debt and don't use your cards, your score will improve because your lower ratio of debt to your available credit will make you appear as though you are more creditworthy. Your score will increase because you will appear as someone who uses credit wisely.

Don't apply for any new loans or credit cards just before you apply for a mortgage. Each time you apply for a new loan your credit score could go down 10 to 20 points, depending on how many outstanding credit cards or loans you already have on the books. Sometimes, people with low balances and few credit cards will see an increase in their credit score of 10 points if they apply for new cards. However, you shouldn't take that risk just before you seek a new major loan, such as a mortgage or car loan.

Scoring Tips

Never get a car loan just before you buy a house. A new major loan will definitely lower your score and will increase the interest rate you are offered on your mortgage. If you need a car, wait until after you close on your house and have your mortgage in place. In fact, a new car loan might make it impossible for you to qualify for a new mortgage because your debt levels are too high.

Correct Big Mistakes

Take a look at your credit report and correct big mistakes, such as someone else's bad credit history. Even if the history shows the bad credit is paid off, a bankruptcy, collection action, or charge-off on your account will lower your credit score significantly. Sometimes an ex-spouse or relative with a similar name will have his or her bad credit history linked with yours. Be sure to get the accounts on which you were not a co-borrower removed from your reports.

If this negative mark is part of your credit history, it will take seven years to get rid of it. Your score will gradually improve as it becomes older and older.

If an account that is yours shows a negative report, such as late payments or collections when an error was made on your bill, ask to have the information corrected. In Chapter 4, I discussed how to correct credit report errors.

Use the Online Dispute Process

One of the fastest ways to get corrections made to your credit report is to use the online dispute process for each of the credit reporting agencies. But be sure you print out everything before hitting that Send button, so you have a copy of what you sent. Also save copies of everything you get from the credit bureau in reply.

Update Positive Accounts

Sometimes you'll find that a positive account is only reporting to one or two of the credit reporting agencies, but not to all three agencies. You'll likely find that you have a higher credit score at the bureaus that have the positive account.

Contact your creditor and ask him to update or report the positive information to the agency that does not have the report. This is most likely to happen with a small bank or loan company that only reports to one credit agency. They may not be willing to help, but it's worth asking.

Scoring Tips

Be sure your credit limits are accurate. Higher credit limits show that you have more available credit, which will improve your credit score.

Also, if you find that your credit limits are reported lower than they actually are, ask for the correction. Often when you first apply for a credit card you are offered a lower credit limit that then gets increased as you pay your bills on time.

Things That Won't Help

Not everything you do to clean up your credit reports is helpful. In fact, some things can make your credit score go down or may even be illegal.

Don't Overdispute

Try not to send more than three or four disputes to the credit reporting agencies at one time. You can file too many disputes at once and be seen as a frivolous filer. Work on the major accounts or major errors first, and then correct any minor fixes.

You may find that if you overdispute even good accounts, the good accounts might be the ones that don't show up again because the reporting company doesn't bother to answer the dispute. If the credit reporting agency does not get a response within 30 days, it will remove the item. Often the companies that don't respond are the ones that don't believe there is a dispute, which will likely be the accounts in good standing. You could end up with a lower credit score because you have fewer positive accounts.

Credit Cautions

Don't pay for credit repair services. They won't help and they could hurt. A favorite tactic of phony credit repair services is to dispute everything. Although this may get some things temporarily off your credit report while it's being investigated, the negative item will return and may even return with more negative information.

Don't Create a New Credit Identity

Credit scam services may recommend that you create a new credit identity. The way they do this is by using a Social Security number from someone who is dead, such as a dead infant.

Another favorite tactic is to tell you to apply for a taxpayer identification number, which is used by the IRS for business accounts. You probably won't find that helpful. Because the business will have no credit history, a creditor will likely ask you for your Social Security number.

Credit Cautions

If someone recommends that you start a new credit identity, find someone else to help you. It is considered credit fraud and you can end up with some serious legal problems.

Although you may be able to pull off one of these frauds, you still won't find any decent credit offers. Neither of these numbers will have a credit history. It will take you years to build a decent credit score and probably won't get you there much faster than just cleaning up your own credit history and paying down debt.

Close Problem Accounts

You may think that just closing accounts in trouble will help improve your score. It won't. Negative accounts can stay on your credit report for seven years, even if they are closed, so closing them won't help.

In fact, closing a problem account might end up lowering your score because it will reduce the amount of your available credit. For example, suppose you have three accounts with a credit limit of $5,000 each for a total of $15,000 available credit. You've charged a total of $8,000. You haven't charged anything to the problem account, so its balance is $500. You won't be able to close that account until the balance is paid off. Suppose you pay it off and close it. You'll then have $7,500 and $10,000 available credit. When you had three accounts opened, you were using 53 percent of your available credit ($8,000/$15,000). After closing the problem account, you'll be using 75 percent of available credit ($7,500/$10,000). Your credit score will go down because you are using a higher percentage of available credit.

Scoring Tips

Yes, it's a good idea to pay off a problem account, but don't close it. Keep your accounts open even if they have a zero balance. They can't hurt you. They'll increase your available credit and, if they are an old account, they'll make your credit history look older.

Your problem account could also be your oldest account. Suppose it was your first credit card. You opened it in 1980. The other two cards with better rates were opened in 2000 and 2004. By closing the oldest card you make your credit history look much younger, which could also lower your credit score.

Pay Off Collection Accounts

Paying off accounts that have been sent to collections should be handled very differently than credit cards or loans for which you just have a few late payments. If you make a payment on a collection account, it just updates the date of activity on that account and may make the negative mark look current. That can actually hurt your credit score. As negative marks age and remain inactive on a credit report, their impact on your credit score gradually decreases.

Although you do want to pay off collection accounts to clean up your credit score, negotiate that payment with a promise to remove the negative mark from your credit score. Let the collection agency know that you will pay off the debt in full if they will remove it from the credit score. Most collection agencies just want the money and will negotiate that type of deal to get it.

Whenever you negotiate with a collection agency, make sure you get everything in writing. An agent can promise anything by telephone and then deny the promise later.

The Least You Need to Know

- If you want to boost your credit score quickly, the best thing you can do is pay off all your credit cards.

- Don't apply for any new loans or credit cards before applying for a mortgage.

- Keep your spending on existing credit cards to a minimum before applying for a major loan.

- Correct any major errors on your credit cards, but don't dispute too much at once.

- Pay off a problem card, but don't close it.

- Pay off a collection account, but only after you negotiate a promise to remove the negative mark from your credit reports—and get it in writing.

Part 3

Getting Through a Scoring Crisis

Life happens and sometimes that means you're going to face a major financial crisis. Although you may not be able to avoid a hit to your credit score, there are things you can do to minimize the damage. In this part, I talk about actions you can take to minimize your credit score damage, as well as how to repair any damage done to your credit score after a crisis.

Chapter 12

Dealing with a Credit Crisis

In This Chapter

- ◆ Looking for cash
- ◆ Prioritizing payments
- ◆ Establishing a plan
- ◆ Getting help
- ◆ Filing bankruptcy

We all face financial crises during our lifetimes. Whether it's a serious illness that makes it impossible for a primary wage earner to work or the loss of a job, in a matter of a month or two you could be facing a debt crisis. You may find the crisis gradually creeping up as your debt levels build until all of a sudden you just can't pay those monthly charges.

If you've been smart and have an emergency savings account in place, you may be able to delay the crisis for several months. In this chapter, I look at what you should do when facing a financial crisis and how to minimize the damage to your credit score.

Finding Cash

Many people live from check to check and maybe have a small savings that can carry them for a month or two. Though I certainly recommend that you build an emergency fund that will cover your bills for at least three months, six months is even better—however, most families find it hard to just meet their monthly payments.

When faced with a debt crisis, don't panic. Take some time to think even as those creditors keep calling. Get a telephone with caller ID and monitor your calls. You don't have to answer the ones from creditors.

Paying the creditor that calls the most may not be your best strategy. Take the time to build a plan that will get your debt under control. Be sure you set your priorities for paying your bills according to what is best for you, not what is best for your creditors.

> **Scoring Tips**
>
> You'll find lots of ideas about how to live more frugally at the Frugal Life website (www.thefrugallife. com). *The Pocket Idiot's Guide to Living on a Budget* (Alpha Books, 1999) may also give you some good ideas about how to manage your money more wisely.

Before you put together a payment plan, your first step is to figure out how much cash you have and how much you could have if you immediately cut back on spending. The big mistake many people make when first faced with a financial crisis is not putting on the spending brakes fast enough.

You may have a car that you just can't afford anymore. Think about selling it and getting something with a lower monthly payment. You may have a cell phone plan that costs too much each month. You could decide to reduce the number of minutes available and just use the phone for emergencies until you get out of the crisis. You may find that you can free up more cash quickly. You may go out to eat a lot. Start cooking at home and you'll be amazed at how much you can save.

As you look for more cash, also take the time to identify your major expenses. Write down every payment you must make each month. Also jot down regular cash spending—such as food shopping, dining out, going out for drinks, and other common cash expenses. Try to make the list as complete as you can.

Circle the items that you could do without and sacrifice little. Eating out is definitely one of those things. You may need to start packing lunches for work. Although you don't want to cut out all entertainment, think of ways to cut costs. Maybe you can rent movies and avoid all the costs of going to a theater. Think of spending a day at the park rather than paying for a more expensive outing.

Add up the cash you found by removing the easy items. You'll probably find that it won't be enough to meet the mounting bills and you'll need to dig deeper.

Next use a different color to circle the items that you could give up, but that will require a bit more sacrifice. Yes, it will be difficult, but isn't it better than losing your house or filing for bankruptcy? Take the hard steps now and pay down your debt. You may find it difficult, but living as frugally as possible for six months to a year may get you out of the debt crisis or give you the opportunity to re-establish yourself after a job loss or illness. The faster you cut back, the less pain you'll feel in the long run.

Add up the items circled in this second group and add the total to the amount found in the first group. This should now give you a significant amount of cash to work with each month. If you still need more, your next step would be to sell things or to find a way to make more money. If you've just lost a job, consider taking on work even if it means working in a fast-food restaurant. You want to at least keep the cash flowing and avoid financial disaster until you can find a job that better suits your skills.

Don't think about debt consolidation, such as taking a second mortgage or equity line to pay off debt. You don't want to make *unsecured debt*, such as money due to credit card companies, and *secure* it against your house. That could put you at a greater risk of losing your house if you can't afford to make the payments.

def•i•ni•tion

Unsecured debt is debt that has not been secured by assets. This includes credit cards and personal loans. **Secured debt** is debt that is secured by assets, such as a mortgage on your house or a loan on your car. If you fail to pay a secured debt, you can lose the asset that was put up as collateral. You can lose a home to foreclosure if you fail to pay the mortgage. You can lose a car to repossession if you fail to pay a car loan. *Foreclosure* is the process in which the financial institution that offered you a mortgage on your home takes possession of the home for failure to make the mortgage payments. *Repossession* is the process in which the financial institution that financed your car takes possession of the car for failure to pay the monthly amount due.

Sorting Out Your Options

After you've figured out how much money you have to work with to pay your bills, you need to figure out the best use of that money. You may find that you just can't pay all the bills. The key will be to figure out which bills to pay, and they probably won't be the bills due to the most annoying credit collectors—the unsecured credit cards.

Your first step in sorting out your options should be prioritizing your bills. Then develop a payment plan. If you can't work out a reasonable plan on your own, then seek outside help. Finally, if all else fails, you may need to protect your biggest asset—your home—by filing bankruptcy.

Bill Prioritization

Make a list of all bills that need to be paid. On top of that list should be your mortgage, if you own a home. That bill should always be the first paid. You want to secure the place you live and not put yourself at risk of losing your home to foreclosure.

Your next most important bill is your car loan. Failure to make that payment could result in the loss of your car. If your car loan can't be paid, think about selling the car before you lose it to repossession. Repossession is a black mark on your credit score that will take a long time to erase. If public transportation is an alternative for a while, use that or buy a car that won't require such a large monthly payment.

Next in line are bills that help keep you alive. You need to eat and you need to pay for essential medical treatments. You may be able to work out a payment plan with the medical facility providing the treatments. Talk with a financial counselor or social worker at the facility. They may even be aware of community or government assistance to help you through a medical crisis.

Utility payments also fit into the category of must-pay bills, so you can keep the lights on, have water, and maintain heating and cooling. If you have both a cell phone and a traditional home phone, think about giving one up to reduce the bills.

Another key bill you must pay is child support, if you have that obligation. Failure to pay child support could result in jail time.

The next group of bills on your list should be ones that could result in wage garnishment—back taxes, court judgments, and student loans. After that you want to pay key insurance bills, such as medical and auto insurance.

Finally, the group of bills that should be at the bottom of your list of priorities should include ones that could hurt your credit score, but won't leave you without a home, car, food, or critical medical care. These include credit cards, department store cards, gas cards, nonessential medical bills, legal bills, and personal loans or loans from family and friends.

Scoring Tips

An excellent tool you can access online to help you develop a repayment plan is the Debt Reduction Planner at Quicken.com (www.quicken.com/planning/debt). Use this tool to help you sort out your debt and come up with a repayment plan. CNN also offers a debt reduction planner that is easy to use at http://cgi.money.cnn.com/tools/debtplanner/debtplanner.jsp.

Developing a Payment Plan

After you've grouped your bills according to priority, make a list on paper with four columns. Column one should be the creditor. Column two should be the reason for paying (for example, the reason for paying your mortgage is to avoid foreclosure). That will help you prioritize the important payments.

Column three should be the amount you usually pay. Column four should be the minimum amount you must pay. For your mortgage and your car loan, columns three and four will likely be the same, but for a credit card you may regularly pay more than the minimum balance due but the minimum due might be considerably less.

Money owed to family and friends would likely have zero in the column of minimum due. You may be embarrassed to admit your financial difficulties, but don't hesitate to talk with family and friends to whom you owe money and ask for a delay in repayment. They will be the easiest ones to put off until after a financial crisis.

Add up column four and see if the cash you've found is enough to cover the minimum due for all outstanding bills. If not, you may need to go back to your list of spending and make more severe sacrifices.

Late payments will swiftly lower your credit score—even one late payment can reduce your score by as much as 100 points. Also, it sends up alarm bells to all your creditors. If your credit card has a provision that permits it to increase your interest even if you are late in payments to another creditor, you could find that your interest rates on all affected cards increase to as high as 30 percent. I talked more about the importance of paying your bills on time in Chapter 7.

Seeking Help

If you just can't find enough money to pay the minimum of your bills due, don't wait to seek help. Get help as soon as you realize you are in over your head. The faster you seek help, the easier it will be for someone to help you. If you wait until you've gotten foreclosure notices and notices of repossession, your only means of stopping them may be bankruptcy.

Some people turn to debt consolidation rather than try to work out another type of payment plan. Don't fall prey to this temptation. You will put your primary asset—your home—at risk. Debt consolidation turns unsecured debt, primarily credit card debt, into debt secured by your home.

Rather than debt consolidation, think about credit counseling. I talk more about how to find the right counselor in Chapter 13. Credit counselors can negotiate with your creditors and often arrange for reductions in interest rates and penalties. They can help you budget and work out a payment plan to get you through a debt crisis.

Scoring Tips

If your home is financed through the FHA, seek the help of a U.S. Department of Housing and Urban Development housing counselor. You can find one near your home by searching its database online at www.hud.gov/offices/hsg/sfh/hcc/hcs.cfm or by calling 1-800-333-4636 to find an office near you. HUD housing counselors can help you with credit counseling, and in many cases their services are free. They will definitely work to help you keep your house.

If debt consolidation becomes an option you must consider, only do so if you decide to destroy all your credit cards and not buy with credit until the equity loan you take is paid off. Don't borrow more than 90 percent of your home value when you add together both your first mortgage and the new debt.

Even though you may find this equity loan gives you a bit of breathing room and offers you a lower interest rate than the credit cards you're paying off, don't stretch out your repayment of the debt. Stop spending and concentrate on getting this debt paid off as quickly as possible.

Throwing in the Towel—Bankruptcy

You may find after trying all these things that your crisis is just too severe and your only alternative is to seek the protection provided by the bankruptcy law. This law allows you to erase unsecured debt provided you meet the stringent provisions of the law.

I talk more about seeking bankruptcy protection, the types of protection available, and how to file bankruptcy in Chapter 14. Bankruptcy puts a cloud on your credit report for 10 years, so only consider this route as a last resort when all else fails. But in many states, you can protect your home from foreclosure with bankruptcy protection provided you can continue to make the mortgage payments. By erasing unsecured debt, you'll have more money to make payments on the secured debt.

The Least You Need to Know

◆ Don't delay in putting a stop to spending if you find yourself facing a debt crisis. The faster you put on the brakes, the better chance you have of surviving the crisis without major damage to your financial situation and your credit score.

◆ Review your spending and find ways to cut back and free up cash so you can pay your bills on time.

◆ Prioritize your bills by their importance, not by which creditor bothers you the most. Pay your secured debt first, then pay your unsecured debt.

◆ Seek professional help as soon as you realize you have a problem. Don't wait until you get notices of foreclosure and repossession.

◆ If all else fails, consider bankruptcy to save your home and car.

Chapter **13**

Seeking Help from Credit Counselors

In This Chapter

- ◆ Discovering credit counseling types
- ◆ Interviewing potential counselors
- ◆ Selecting the best counseling for you
- ◆ Reviewing what to expect

You should never hesitate to seek help from a credit counselor if your bills are piling up and you just can't seem to get a handle on them. An objective third person can help you sort out the problem and figure out what your best alternatives are for finding your way out of a credit mess.

In this chapter, I review the different types of credit counseling services available, tell you how to find the best counselor for you, and review what you can expect when you hire a counselor.

Exploring Types of Credit Counselors

You'll find four different types of counselors available to you:

◆ Credit counselors

◆ Debt negotiation specialists

◆ Debt consolidation specialists

◆ Debt repair services

Credit Counselors

These counselors offer a full range of services including advice on how to manage your money better, solutions for your current financial problems, and help in developing a personalized plan that you can use to prevent future difficulties. Good ones can offer you *debt management plans*, money management education, and homeowner counseling and education. Often these counselors not only help you come up with a plan for repaying your debt, they also contact your creditors and negotiate lower interest rates. When these rates are in place, they help you develop a repayment plan so you no longer get harassing calls.

def•i•ni•tion

A **debt management plan** is a systematic way to pay down your debt. You need to have enough income to make the payments for a debt management plan to work.

Debt Negotiation Specialists

These specialists focus solely on negotiating settlements with your creditors. While they're negotiating these payoff settlements, they collect money from you on a monthly basis that is used to pay your creditors when a settlement amount is reached. Debt negotiation specialists can be a very risky choice and can have a long-term negative impact on your credit report and your ability to get credit in the future. Fraudulent ones collect money and pocket it. Many states have laws regulating debt negotiation companies and the services they offer. Before signing a contract with a debt negotiation company, be sure to contact your state attorney general for more information about these laws.

Debt Consolidation Specialists

This type of counselor can include a specialist at many different types of financial institutions including your own bank. But you should be careful before considering debt consolidation. If you consolidate your credit card debt to reduce your monthly payment, you will be converting unsecured debt (which can be discharged in a bankruptcy) with secured debt against your home. You may be putting your home at greater risk and just stalling the inevitable. You should only consider a consolidation loan if you truly plan to pay down that debt before starting to charge on your credit cards again. The costs of consolidation loans can also add up. You may have to pay points, which is 1 percent of the amount you want to borrow, as well as other closing costs. These types of loans offer a tax advantage because their interest is tax deductible, although the interest paid to credit card companies is not tax deductible.

Debt Repair Services

These are not truly debt counselors, nor do they offer a legitimate service. In fact, you could be getting yourself into legal trouble. There is no simple route to repairing your credit. Follow the steps in Chapter 15 to rebuild your credit after a credit crisis. You can do it on your own more effectively and legally.

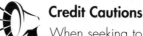 **Credit Cautions**

When seeking to hire a credit counselor, be skeptical of any counselor who promises to fix your credit report or score and settle your debt for very little money. If it sounds too good to be true, it probably is.

Knowing What to Ask When Picking a Counselor

When you start searching for a credit counselor, the following are the key questions you should ask:

◆ Is your credit counseling agency a nonprofit organization? If the agency answers no, just hang up and move on. You definitely should not work with a credit counseling agency that is a for-profit organization.

- Will you inform me of all fees associated with the services being offered? If the counselor dances around this topic and hesitates giving you a fee schedule, be very skeptical.

- Are all the services your agency offers confidential? This should be yes in all cases.

- Does your agency offer plans tailored to my needs or do you offer the same plan to everyone? You definitely want an agency that takes the time to figure out your family's individual needs and then devises a plan that works for you.

- Are your counselors certified and your agency accredited? You definitely want to work with a counselor and agency that has been certified and accredited by the National Foundation for Credit Counselors (NFCC). You can find out more about them at www. nfcc.org.

- Do you offer budget and credit education opportunities? You definitely want to find an agency that offers more than just a way to pay off your debt. You want an agency that will help you with credit and debt education and will help prevent you from getting into trouble again.

- Will funds that you collect from me be protected? The agency should be able to tell you how they handle funds collected from you and what protections are offered for those funds. Be sure that all payments you send as part of your debt management plan are sent to creditors in a timely manner. Some agencies may collect your first month's payment and call it a fee or donation and not send any money to your creditors. Ask the counselor how quickly they disburse your funds to your creditors.

Credit Cautions

Don't work with a credit counselor who collects your first payment as a fee or who delays payments to creditors. I talk more about fees to expect in the following sections.

Picking the Right Counselor for You

Finding the right counselor will be crucial to your success. You not only want to check out the legitimacy of the agency, but you also want to be sure that the counselor is someone you can easily work with. You'll find it much harder to share your most intimate financial details with a person that you just don't feel comfortable talking to.

As you ask the key questions from the previous section, gauge how comfortable you would feel discussing your personal situation with the counselor. If the agency advertised they were a nonprofit agency, but the counselor seems more concerned about collecting their fees than finding out about you, seek another agency.

Your counselor should be talking to you about their full range of services, not pushing to collect money from you. These services should include a comprehensive budget review and a range of recommendations specific to your needs, not just a debt management plan designed to pay down your credit cards.

> **Scoring Tips**
>
> You can find accredited credit counselors affiliated with the NFCC at www. debtadvice.org. Some agencies offer free budget counseling and debt management services, others offer services at fees or contributions that are affordable for consumers in debt.

Some credit agencies can offer their services for free, others charge minimal fees. If they do charge fees, here is a fee structure suggested by the NFCC:

♦ Educational seminars are free and open to the public at most NFCC agencies.

♦ Most agencies can provide housing and mortgage counseling at no charge because they are funded by the U.S. Department of Housing.

♦ One-on-one budget counseling should be offered for an average of $13.

♦ If you enroll in a debt management plan, the total average monthly fees are $14 plus an average start-up fee of $23. Many times a debt management plan can even be offered for free because the creditors contribute to the NFCC agencies. If you are quoted higher fees, then contact a different agency or the NFCC national office at 1-800-388-2227.

Be sure that your sessions with the counselor are substantive and that the counselor truly takes the time to understand your personal financial situation. For example, NFCC counselors usually spend about 90 minutes on the initial counseling appointment.

Discovering What to Expect During Counseling

The first step during any counseling program should be a comprehensive discussion about your current financial situation. Bring information about all your bills and any collection activities that currently involve you or any family member to your first counseling session.

You should expect a full range of services including comprehensive budget planning, debt management plans, money management education, and homeowner counseling and education. If the only service an agency offers is a debt management plan, say no and find another agency.

After the comprehensive review of your current debt situation, the credit counselor will discuss numerous alternatives for getting you back on track, including budget management and money management education. If your debt situation is very severe, the counselor may recommend a debt management plan as your best option for returning to financial health.

A debt management plan is a systematic way to pay down your debt. You need to have enough income to make the payments for a debt management plan to work. If your income is too low, the agency may recommend bankruptcy. At that point the agency will give you a certificate for the bankruptcy court (provided they are a counseling agency approved by the bankruptcy court) so you can file your case. I talk more about bankruptcy in Chapter 14.

If you enter into a debt management plan, you will be required to make monthly payments to the agency. The agency will then distribute these funds to your creditors. By agreeing to participate in a debt management plan, your finance charges may be reduced or waived and your collection calls will be reduced. Some creditors may refuse to work with the credit counseling agency and will continue to call you.

It usually takes about 36 to 60 months to repay debts through a debt management plan. The time it takes will depend on how much you owe and how much cash you have available to make the payments. An NFCC credit counseling agency will work with all your creditors, even if the creditors decide not to make a contribution to the agency.

When you successfully complete the plan, the credit counseling agency will help you re-establish your credit. This can include helping you get a car loan—if you need a new car—or a home mortgage, if you have the income and are ready to buy a home. Throughout the debt management plan, the credit counselor will help you rebuild a positive credit history and an improved credit score.

The Least You Need to Know

+ There are four types of credit counselors, but you should only work with a counselor that is certified and an agency that is affiliated with the NFCC.

+ You should never work with a credit agency that uses your first payment as part of its fees.

+ You should expect more than a debt management plan from your credit counselor. You should also be offered credit education and budget services.

+ Be sure you click with your counselor. You won't be able to discuss your intimate financial details with a counselor you don't feel comfortable talking to.

+ If you complete a debt management plan working with a certified credit counselor, you will get help in re-establishing your credit.

Chapter 14

Considering Bankruptcy

In This Chapter

- ◆ Knowing the types
- ◆ Following the filing steps
- ◆ Selecting the best bankruptcy option
- ◆ Reviewing bankruptcy's effects on your credit score

Sometimes you're just in too deep and you don't have the income available to pay off all your debt. After exploring your payoff options with a credit counselor as discussed in Chapter 13, your only option may be bankruptcy.

Bankruptcy used to be the type of black mark that would destroy all chances of you getting credit again for 10 years or more. Luckily, today the negative consequences are not that bad.

Bankruptcy gives you a chance for a fresh financial start. In this chapter, I review the types of bankruptcies, how you file, and how a bankruptcy impacts your credit score.

Reviewing Types of Bankruptcies

Bankruptcy comes in four key types, but only two that are commonly filed by individuals. The bankruptcy types include the following:

◆ Chapter 7. In this type of bankruptcy, you ask the bankruptcy court to discharge all your debts, which means any unsecured credit will be wiped out to zero dollars. But if you have secured debts, such as the mortgage on your home or loan on your car, you will have to give up your property to discharge that debt. You will be able to keep certain income benefits such as Social Security, unemployment compensation, veteran's benefits, public assistance, and pensions. These types of income will not fall under the control of the bankruptcy court. The exemption amounts are doubled if a married couple files together.

◆ Chapter 11. This type of bankruptcy is used primarily by businesses so they can stop their creditors from collecting and have time to reorganize their debts. Individuals who consider using Chapter 11 bankruptcy must have assets above one or both of the Chapter 13 bankruptcy limits, which are unsecured debts of more than $307,675 or secured debts of more than $922,975. You can also use Chapter 11 if your assets are above both debt levels.

◆ Chapter 12. This type of bankruptcy is very similar to Chapter 13 bankruptcy, but 80 percent of the debt must come from operating a family farm. If you own a family farm, you should hire an attorney to help you through the process of Chapter 12 bankruptcy. The attorney should be someone who knows the laws specific to Chapter 12 bankruptcy filing and who can best help you protect your property and possibly save your farm with a restructuring of your debt.

◆ Chapter 13. In this type of bankruptcy, you must show how you will pay off some of your past due and current debts during a period of three to five years. You will be allowed to keep your most valuable property, especially your home and car. In most cases, you will be required to make payments that are at least as much as your regular monthly payments on your mortgage and car loan with some extra payments to get caught up on the amount that is past due. You must have enough income to pay for your necessities and to keep up with the required payments as they come due. The bankruptcy court will set a monthly payment that you make to the trustee and then the trustee will pay your creditors.

Understanding the Steps for Filing

I will focus on the two most common bankruptcies filed by individuals: Chapter 7 and Chapter 13. The process for a Chapter 12 bankruptcy is very similar to that of a Chapter 13, but you should use Chapter 12 only if you have a family farm. Chapter 11 is much more expensive and complex. You definitely should not try to file that one on your own.

Chapter 7 Bankruptcy

Chapter 7 bankruptcy might sound like the best. You can erase all your debt with no payments. It's actually not quite that easy and you could lose your house and car.

Your first step to see if you qualify for a Chapter 7 bankruptcy is a debt and income test. Your debts must be primarily from consumer spending rather than spending for your business. Your average monthly income must be either at or below the median income for your state.

 Scoring Tips

You can find the median income for your state at the census bureau website: http://quickfacts.census.gov/qfd/. Historically, 85 percent of the people who file for Chapter 7 bankruptcy fall below these income limits.

If your monthly income is higher than the state's family median income and your debts are primarily from consumer spending, you will need to take a means test to see if you qualify to file for Chapter 7. The four steps of a means test are as follows:

1. **Calculate your current monthly income.**

2. **Subtract certain allowable IRS expense amounts.** There are numerous charts for each type of expense published by the IRS. You can find the allowable expenses based on the size of your

family for food, clothing, housekeeping supplies, personal care, transportation, utilities, and other miscellaneous expenses at www.usdoj.gov/ust/eo/bapcpa/20061001/meanstesting.htm.

3. **Calculate your monthly projected disposable income.** If the income left over after subtracting the IRS-allowable expenses is $100 or more, you will need to figure out your monthly disposable income.

4. **Calculate your monthly disposable income, if necessary.** First subtract all your mandatory debts for all secured credit, such as your mortgage and your car payments. If you have more than $100 left, that is considered disposable income and will be used to repay your unsecured debt. If you can pay off 25 percent of your total unsecured debt with that disposable income, then you likely would not be eligible for a Chapter 7 bankruptcy and would have to file a Chapter 13 bankruptcy.

If you pass the means test, you will then need to seek credit counseling from a nonprofit credit counseling agency approved by the bankruptcy trustee. The agency will determine whether it is feasible for you to pay off your debts outside of bankruptcy without adding to what you owe.

Scoring Tips

You must seek credit counseling before applying for bankruptcy. You can find out more about credit counseling and the approved agencies at U.S. Trustee website at www.usdoj.gov/ust/eo/bapcpa/ccde/index.htm.

You will need to provide the bankruptcy trustee for your region proof that you received credit counseling within a 180-day period before filing for bankruptcy. After you're finished working with the agency, you will receive a certificate showing that you participated in counseling. The agency will also give you a copy of any repayment plan worked out during the counseling.

You can file a bankruptcy case pro se, which means without the assistance of an attorney, but the U.S. Bankruptcy Court will make it very clear that it is extremely difficult to do so successfully. Professional advice from an attorney can help protect your rights, because bankruptcy is a very complicated legal proceeding and you can be certain your creditors will have attorneys to question the discharge of your debt. Even if you decide to file bankruptcy without an attorney, you should at least seek legal advice before filing to be sure you are completing the paperwork correctly and taking all the proper steps.

When you set up an appointment with an attorney, check on the fees for the appointment. Many attorneys will not charge for the brief initial consultation. Bankruptcy attorneys must disclose all their fees and can only take your case after you have signed a writ-

Scoring Tips

You can find a bankruptcy attorney by asking family and friends, but if no one knows a good attorney to recommend, you can find one through an online directory at the National Association of Consumer Bankruptcy Attorneys (www.nacba.org). When you get to the home page, click the link at the top right entitled "Attorney Finder."

ten contract. If you can't afford to pay a bankruptcy attorney, you may be able to find free or low-cost legal services through your local or state bar association or country courthouse. You can also look under "Legal Aid" or "Legal Assistance" in the yellow pages of your phone book. If all attempts fail locally, there is a state-by-state directory at the Legal Services Corporation website (www.lsc.gov). When you get to the website, look for a link at the top right called "Find Legal Assistance."

You must file your bankruptcy case in the U.S. Bankruptcy Court Division nearest to where you live. You can find the closest court on the U.S. Trustee Program website (www.usdoj.gov/ust/index.htm). You can also find links to download all the forms you need to file for bankruptcy at that website.

If the court approves your bankruptcy filing under Chapter 7, the court will discharge most of your debts including the following:

- ◆ Bank credit cards

- ◆ Utility bills

- ◆ Doctor and hospital bills

- ◆ Personal loans

- ◆ Department or other retail store credit cards

- ◆ Mail order and catalog purchases

Credit Cautions

Be very careful when you make a listing of your debt. For the court to discharge your debt, you must list the debt when you file the bankruptcy. If you forget to list a debt, you have to pay it back after the bankruptcy.

- Loan balances due on loan deficiencies, such as repossessed automobiles or houses lost to foreclosure

- Most lawsuit judgments

- Obligations under leases and contracts

You can't get all your debt discharged. There are some types of debt the bankruptcy court will not discharge. These debts include the following:

- Student loans

- Domestic support obligations, such as child support and alimony

- Fines imposed by governmental entities for breaking the law

- Income taxes imposed because you did not file a return or were intentionally avoiding your taxes

- Business-related taxes, such as payroll taxes, excise taxes, sales taxes, use taxes, poll taxes, and customs duties

- Debts incurred through fraud or willful and malicious injury

- Debts incurred as the result of a death or personal injury caused by you when driving your car while under the influence of alcohol or other illegal substance

When you file a Chapter 7 bankruptcy, any property secured by a mortgage, deed of trust, promissory note, or other instrument is at risk. If you are able to continue making the payments after the bankruptcy, you likely will be able to keep your home and car, as long as the court considers that property necessary. But if you can't afford to make the payments and keep your mortgage or car loan current, the bankruptcy will not save your property. Bankruptcy filing will only delay the foreclosure until the case is completed or the court lifts the stay on the foreclosure.

Some of your other property may be exempt. Federal and state exemption systems exist to exclude some of the equity in your property. In some states the exemption amounts are higher and you can choose to go by those amounts. In other states you can only choose to use the state exemption amounts. Anything you own with a value above the exempted amounts will be sold to pay your creditors.

Filing for a Chapter 7 bankruptcy is not free. You will pay a fee of $274 to file. If you can't afford to pay the fee, you can ask for a fee waiver or for permission to pay in installments. In addition to paying the filing fees, you will also need to pay an attorney, which can range between $1,000 and $2,000. Although you can file a bankruptcy case without the help of an attorney, it is definitely wise to hire one to help you through the maze of this very difficult process.

Scoring Tips

You can find out about the rules for personal bankruptcy and exemptions in your state at www. bankruptcyinformation.com/ services.html.

You will also need to pay the costs of copying almost all your financial records including past tax returns, paycheck stubs, payment demands, mortgages, deeds, summonses, court judgments, credit card statements, medical bills, bank account statements, child support or alimony agreements, student loans, and any documentation of any past bankruptcies. In addition to these costs, you will need to take off from work and attend at least one meeting with the bankruptcy trustee. If your creditors challenge the discharge of debts, more than one meeting may be required and you could end up with a hearing before a bankruptcy judge.

As soon as your bankruptcy is filed, the court will set a date for a meeting of creditors. You must appear at this meeting, but it probably won't take place in a courtroom. Often the meeting is held at a hearing room in the federal building at which the bankruptcy court is located. The meeting is run by the bankruptcy trustee, not by a judge.

During this meeting the bankruptcy trustee and your creditors can ask questions about the financial information included in the filing and about other issues they believe are relevant to the bankruptcy filing and your ability to pay the debt. For example, you may be asked about expected tax refunds; recent large payments made to other creditors, family members, or friends; any documents that may be missing; and any inconsistencies in the information provided. If you aren't represented by a lawyer, you will probably face stiffer questioning about the information provided and how you calculated property exemptions.

Creditors rarely show up at these meetings, and most of the questions will come from the bankruptcy trustee. If the paperwork you submitted is complete and well prepared, the questions will be brief and the meeting quick and relatively painless.

The primary reason creditors might object is if they believe the debts you incurred were the result of a fraudulent act. For example, if you go out and run up a lot of debt just before filing for bankruptcy, that could be considered fraudulent behavior. Also, if the creditor believes you made false statements to get a loan, he could challenge the charge off of the debt.

In most Chapter 7 bankruptcies a judge will not be involved, but if an issue is contested you will need to appear before a judge. Some key issues that can be contested include the following:

♦ Your income level appears too high for Chapter 7 and you want to ask for an exception because of special circumstances.

♦ One of your creditors contests your right to file a Chapter 7 bankruptcy or discharge a particular debt.

♦ You want to ask a judge to discharge a debt that is not normally discharged in a Chapter 7 bankruptcy, such as a student loan or past-due taxes.

♦ You want to eliminate a lien on your property that would otherwise survive a bankruptcy without a ruling from a judge.

♦ You are handling your own bankruptcy without the help of an attorney and want to keep making payments on your car or home. This is called reaffirming the debt.

Your Chapter 7 bankruptcy will end with the discharge of all debts that are eligible to be discharged. When your debt is discharged, your creditor can never try to collect it from you again or report it to a credit bureau as an ongoing debt. Your credit report will likely show the debt as discharged by bankruptcy, but the creditor cannot indicate that you still owe the money or are past due on payments.

You can decide to change your mind before the debt is discharged and withdraw your bankruptcy filing. In most cases the court will do so without a problem, unless your withdrawal is not in the best interest of your creditors. The trustee may oppose the withdrawal of your case if your nonexempt assets could be sold to pay your creditors.

If you decide to withdraw your case, you can file again later, but you may have to wait at least 180 days to do so and pay a new filing fee. You also have the option of converting your case into another type of bankruptcy such as a Chapter 13, which people will sometimes decide they want to do to save property that may otherwise be sold to pay creditors.

Chapter 13 Bankruptcy

You start a Chapter 13 bankruptcy by filling out a package of forms very similar to those you must complete for a Chapter 7 bankruptcy. You can find the forms you need and download them at the U.S. Trustee Program website (www.usdoj.gov/ust/index.htm). Unlike a Chapter 7 bankruptcy, you don't have to pass a means test or seek credit counseling first, but it is a good idea. The counselor will help you develop a repayment plan that will likely be used by the bankruptcy trustee.

The key difference between a Chapter 7 and a Chapter 13 bankruptcy is that in addition to the forms you must complete for a Chapter 7 bankruptcy, you must also …

- Prepare a workable plan to repay some or all your debts during the plan period, which can be either three or five years depending on your income. If your income is below the state's median income, then you can submit a three-year plan. If it's above the state's median income, then you must submit a five-year plan. Some creditors must receive 100 percent of what you owe them, while others receive a smaller percentage or possibly nothing at all if you won't have enough disposable income left to pay them after the mandatory debts are paid, such as your mortgage, car payment, or child support.

- Prove that you've filed your federal and state income tax returns for the previous four years.

- Submit your income tax return for the previous year.

You can have all remaining debt discharged after you successfully complete your three- or five-year plan. The repayment plan is one that you propose when you file for Chapter 13 and is amended after the bankruptcy trustee reviews the plan and agrees to what you submit or changes it after receiving all the necessary information. To have your remaining debts discharged that will not be paid during the period of time you are in a repayment plan, you must make all payments required by your plan.

In addition to making all payments, to successfully complete a Chapter 13 repayment plan you must also …

♦ Be current on your federal and state income taxes.

♦ Remain current on any child support or alimony obligations.

♦ File your annual federal income tax return with the court.

♦ File an annual income and expense statement with the court.

You also must provide your creditors with the copies of the income tax returns you file with the court, if they request a copy.

After you've completed your three-year or five-year plan, all remaining unpaid debts will be discharged by the court unless a creditor challenges the discharge of the debt. A judge would then have to look at the facts and determine whether the debt can be discharged. In most cases credit card bills, medical bills, and legal debts can be discharged as well as most court judgments and loans.

You cannot ask to discharge court-imposed fines, back child support and alimony, student loans, recent back taxes, unfiled taxes, or debts that you incurred from a civil judgment that arose from willful or malicious acts (such as causing injury or death from drunk driving). Debts that you cannot discharge will survive the bankruptcy and you will still be obligated to them.

All property secured by a mortgage, deed of trust, or promissory note is at risk if you can't continue to make the required payments. You are not required to give up property that you own in a Chapter 13 bankruptcy, but would be in Chapter 7. The court will not force the sale of property to pay your unsecured debts.

You will be able to keep your house and car as long as you can stay current on your payments. As part of your payment plan you can also pay off any past-due payments, interest, and legal fees incurred. Chapter 13 is the remedy of choice if you are facing foreclosure on your home.

You have to pay a fee to file a Chapter 13 bankruptcy. The cost of filing for a Chapter 13 bankruptcy is $189. If you can't afford the fee, you can apply for a waiver of the fee. You are best seeking legal advice when filing for bankruptcy, but that can get very expensive with a Chapter 13.

Legal costs for a Chapter 13 bankruptcy usually range between $2,500 and $4,000. An attorney who knows the bankruptcy law can help you protect your rights and can work with you to get the best repayment arrangement and save your property.

You can decide to handle the case on your own and save money, but you will still need to pay for some services. You definitely should get some self-help law books. You also should plan to seek some legal help by telephone as you prepare the paperwork, which usually costs about $100 an hour. You should also seek help with the bankruptcy filing forms from someone who specializes in bankruptcy petition preparation, which can range from $300 to $600.

Usually about a month after you file your Chapter 13 bankruptcy petition, the court will schedule a meeting of the creditors. When scheduled, the court will send an official notice of the bankruptcy filing and the meeting to you and all your creditors.

In most cases these meetings last only about 15 minutes, provided you filed complete and accurate information. The bankruptcy trustee will lead the meeting and ask most of the questions. A judge will not be present at this meeting.

The primary purpose of this meeting is to review your repayment plan for its fairness and its legality, as well as your ability to make the payments you proposed. The trustee has a vested interest in your success because he gets a percentage of all payments doled out to creditors to be paid as part of your repayment plan. The trustee will also make sure you've filed and paid your taxes for the past four years. If you haven't, he'll put off the meeting to give you time to file and pay your taxes. You can't proceed with a Chapter 13 repayment plan without your tax filings being up-to-date.

The trustee probably will ask most of the questions, but your creditors may come and question certain aspects of your repayment plan if they don't think the plan is reasonable. The unsecured creditors, who likely get very little under the plan, may question your calculation of disposable income and push for an increase of that disposable income.

Expect to find upset creditors at the meeting. You may even need to modify the plan to appease them and resubmit the plan before your confirmation hearing before the judge. All Chapter 13 filers must make at least one appearance before a bankruptcy judge, which is called the confirmation hearing. He can either confirm your proposed repayment plan or he can reject it and ask you to make changes. Most times if the plan is rejected it will be because you don't have enough disposable income to pay your priority creditors and stay current on your secured debts. You can continue to modify the plan until the judge approves it or decides it is hopeless. Each time you amend the plan, you must go through another confirmation hearing.

A judge can rule on the value of an asset (if the creditor believes it's worth more than you think it's worth); he can rule on a creditor or trustee's objection to parts of your plan; he can rule on whether a debt should be discharged if questioned by a creditor; he can eliminate a lien on your property or decide that it will survive bankruptcy; and he can reaffirm a contract, such as your mortgage, so you can keep your home. If the judge rules Chapter 13 is hopeless, you can switch to a Chapter 7 bankruptcy, but you won't be able to keep your house unless you can make the mortgage payments.

A Chapter 13 case ends when you complete your repayment plan in three to five years, are current on your income tax returns, are current on your child support or alimony payments, and have completed a budget management course approved by the trustee. Any remaining debt that qualifies will be wiped out. Any remaining debt that doesn't qualify to be wiped out will still need to be paid.

You need to live strictly within your means throughout the entire time of the repayment period. The trustee will not allow you to spend money on anything he deems nonessential, and he will be the final word on what is essential.

You can't get the benefits of discharge until you successfully complete the repayment plan. If you don't succeed, you may be able to file for Chapter 7 bankruptcy. Historically, only about 35 percent of Chapter 13 filers make it to the end and get their remaining debts discharged.

If you can't complete the plan on time, you can ask for further modification of the plan. As long as you continue to show good faith that you want to be responsible, the court will consider modifications to the repayment plan. You will need to keep the trustee on your side. He will be the one that the judge will look to when considering modifications and deciding whether to confirm the modified plan.

If you can't continue to make payments into your plan for reasons beyond your control, such as job loss or a medical emergency, a judge might let you end your case early and discharge the remaining debt on the basis of hardship. If you can't get a hardship discharge, you can file for Chapter 7 bankruptcy.

If you end up filing a Chapter 7 bankruptcy, all the money you paid into the Chapter 13 repayment plan will be for nothing. The judge also has the option to dismiss your case, and then you owe all the debt you did before filing for bankruptcy.

Picking the Best Bankruptcy Option for You

After reading all these details, you may be confused about which bank-ruptcy is best for you. If your income is higher than the state's median family income, you won't have a choice to make. You will have to file Chapter 13, unless most of the outstanding debt is related to your busi-ness. If it's mostly business debt, you can choose to file a Chapter 11 bankruptcy. If your debt is primarily from your family farm, you can choose to file Chapter 12.

Otherwise, you'll probably want to file Chapter 7 and have your debt discharged without having to pay any of your unsecured debt. That's because Chapter 7 is faster and easier to file and you don't have to make any payments over time. In most cases, a Chapter 7 case can be opened and closed in three to six months and you emerge debt-free except for mortgage and car loans plus any other debt that is not eli-gible for a discharge.

Few Chapter 7 filers lose any property in Chapter 7 bankruptcy, because state and federal exemption rules allow them to keep most necessities. The new bankruptcy law that passed in October 2005 might make it harder for people to keep all their property with a Chapter 7 bankruptcy. Under the new law property must be valued at its replace-ment value, which could make it harder to meet the limits set in the exemption rules.

Exploring How Bankruptcy Impacts Your Credit Score

Bankruptcy will devastate your credit score. Your score likely already is pretty low because of the negative marks for late payments, repossessions, foreclosures, or other mishaps as your financial situation worsened. A bankruptcy likely will send that credit score even lower by 100 to 150 points and will stay on your credit report for 10 years.

There is good news, though. Usually, 12 months to 2 years after completion of a bankruptcy you will be able to get credit again. In Chapter 15, I talk about how to rebuild your credit after a financial crisis.

The Least You Need to Know

- ◆ You can file one of four different types of bankruptcies—Chapter 7, Chapter 11, Chapter 12, or Chapter 13.

- ◆ A Chapter 7 bankruptcy can wipe out your debt and you won't have to pay any of your unsecured creditors.

- ◆ A Chapter 13 bankruptcy requires you to complete a repayment plan.

- ◆ If you want to save some assets, you may have to file a Chapter 13 bankruptcy. A Chapter 7 bankruptcy trustee or judge could require the sale of all your assets, including your home in some states.

- ◆ Bankruptcy will destroy your credit score initially and stay on your credit report for 10 years, but you'll be able to start getting credit again in about 12 months to 2 years after completing the bankruptcy court's requirements.

Chapter 15

Rebuilding Your Credit Score After the Crisis

In This Chapter

- ◆ Fixing your credit report
- ◆ Coping with unpaid debts
- ◆ Finding limits
- ◆ Looking for positives

After a credit crisis, you'll probably find that your credit report contains late payments and collection actions. You may even have repossession, foreclosure, or possibly a bankruptcy. All these will lower your credit score.

You may be turned down by several lenders and give up, thinking you will never be able to get a loan again, buy a house, or buy a car. Well that's not true, but you will need to work hard at rebuilding your credit score and being able to again get decent interest rates for loans and credit cards.

In this chapter, I show you how to repair your credit, deal with any unpaid debts, explore the legal limits of your bad credit history, and give you hints about how to live a financially healthier life.

Repairing Your Credit Report

First, you must deal with the bad news. You might be terrified of looking at your credit report, but you need to bite the bullet and take a look. Your report may be better than you expect, but even if it looks like a disaster area you shouldn't just give up.

The good news is that the bad credit history won't be around forever. Every type of negative report can only remain on your credit report for a limited amount of time. Here is the maximum time a negative mark can stay on your credit report:

- Late payments—These can be on your report for up to seven years from the time the most recent late payment was reported. If you find late payments on accounts that weren't late or that involved a dispute about a bill, you should ask for a correction if it involves the most recent late payments.

- Collections—If any of your creditors sent your account to a collection agency for collection, you'll likely find that the collection agency also reported the debt. A collection agency action can stay on your credit report for up to seven years from the time the debt was first assigned to the collection agency.

- Court judgments—If a court made a ruling against you that involves a debt, that judgment can stay on your credit report for up to seven years from the date the court filed the ruling.

- Tax liens—If you had a tax lien and paid it off, the lien can remain on your credit report for up to seven years from the date paid. If you don't pay off a tax lien, it can remain on your credit report indefinitely.

Credit Cautions

Don't hire a credit repair specialist who says he can erase these negative marks for you and get you a clean credit report. There is no legal way to get these items removed from your credit report if the information is accurate and can be proven by the creditor or collection agency.

◆ Bankruptcies—If you file for Chapter 7 bankruptcy, it can remain on your credit report for up to 10 years from the date filed for bankruptcy. If you successfully complete a Chapter 13 bankruptcy, it can remain on your credit report for seven years from the date you filed the bankruptcy. I talked more about filing bankruptcy in Chapter 14.

After reading about how long this information stays on your credit history, you might think you need to give up seeking credit for at least seven years. That's not true. As you add positive information and the negative information ages, your credit score will gradually improve.

Correct Errors

Even if your report looks bad, you need to be certain all the information is accurate. I talk about how to correct that information in Chapter 4. In this chapter, I focus on the types of errors you may find that need to be corrected if you've recently been through a financial crisis:

◆ Collection agency "re-aged" your debt—This is a favorite game collection agencies like to play to keep your credit score low and to keep debt looking new. Remember that I said as the debt gets older it has less of an impact on your credit score? Some collection agencies want to keep the pressure on to get you to pay, so they re-age the date by making it look more recent than it actually is. Legally, the collection agency action can only be reported for seven years from the time the agency first reported the debt. Keep a record of that first report and the date it was made. If you see that date changed or that a new collection agency is reporting the same debt, send proof of that to the credit reporting agency and ask for your report to be corrected.

◆ Old delinquencies—If you see late payments or accounts listed as delinquent that are more than seven years old or that don't include the dates of the delinquencies, write to the credit reporting agency and ask for your record to be corrected.

◆ Bankruptcy—If you filed bankruptcy and you see that the type of bankruptcy is not listed on the report, send proof of the type of bankruptcy and ask that the record be corrected. This can be critical if you filed a Chapter 13 bankruptcy because that must be removed seven years from the date you filed for bankruptcy as long as you successfully complete the bankruptcy. However, a Chapter 7 bankruptcy can stay on your record for 10 years. If the bankruptcy is on your record for longer than allowed, ask for it to be removed.

◆ Paid-off debts—If you paid off debts that are listed as unpaid, send proof of the payoff and ask for the record to be corrected.

◆ Accounts included in bankruptcy—If you filed for bankruptcy and there are accounts listed as past due that were included in the bankruptcy, ask that your credit report be corrected to indicate that the account was included in the bankruptcy. Some creditors will continue to list those accounts as past due and update them periodically to keep the negative mark on your credit report longer. That is not legal and you can stop them by having the "included in bankruptcy" added to your report.

◆ Multiple accounts for same debt—Sometimes more than one collection agency or both the collection agency and the original creditor will report to the credit reporting agencies. If you see more than one report regarding the same debt, send proof to the credit reporting agencies and ask for them to correct your credit report.

◆ Accounts or delinquencies that aren't yours—If there are accounts or delinquencies that show on your credit report that are not yours, ask that they be removed. This can be a difficult situation if you were recently involved in a divorce and some of the accounts on your credit report are not yours. You can only ask for the removal of an account if you are not a co-signer of that account.

The good news is that credit-scoring formulas give more weight to your most recent credit history, so if you can build a positive credit history in two to three years, you'll start to see a significant improvement in your ability to get credit and to get better interest rate offers.

The key is to be sure the old stuff is properly dated and will get removed from your report as soon as legally allowed. When you order a report from the credit bureau, you should see a note regarding when that information will be removed. You need to be the policeman of your credit report. No one else will catch unscrupulous creditors using illegal ways to keep a negative mark active and up-to-date.

Planning Your Fix

After scrutinizing your report, make a list using two columns. One column should include all the errors you discover. This should include accounts that are not legitimately yours. Any accounts that include the previously mentioned errors can be included in this column. The second column should include accounts that are legitimately yours and unpaid.

As you start to write to the credit reporting agencies to correct errors, start with accounts in column one that have errors and are paid off. This should include accounts you paid off, accounts included in a bankruptcy, and accounts that aren't yours.

You should only dispute three to four accounts at a time. Credit reporting agencies don't make any money working on corrections, so they don't like to handle them. You'll get better and quicker attention by not over-reporting. After the first group of account corrections are done, then start working on another set of three or four accounts. In Chapter 18, I talk about your rights when correcting your credit report.

Dealing with Unpaid Debts

You should work on repairing the accounts that you still need to pay last, but keep a record of when these accounts were first reported to the credit bureaus. If a creditor tries to change the date first reported, you'll have proof of that action. Remember collection agency records get removed seven years after the agency first reports the collection, so you don't want that date to look more recent than it is.

Rules are different for correcting errors for debts that are still valid, unpaid debts. If the debt involves the original creditor, you should correct any dates that are not accurate. The account, if not paid, drops off your credit report seven years after the most recent late payment was reported. In many cases, if you stop paying a credit card it will eventually be sent to a collection agency.

If any of your accounts on your credit report that are unpaid involve a collection agency, then you should ask the agency to validate the debt. Although other items on your credit report are validated by the credit reporting agency by seeking information from the creditor and deciding who they believe is right or wrong, collection agency debt is validated differently.

When a collection agency is asked to validate debt, they must prove that the debt is your responsibility and that they have a legal right to collect it from you. This can be a very involved process. While the collection agency is pulling together the information required, the collector must cease all collection activity and they must stop reporting it to the credit reporting agencies. It will drop off your credit report while this is going on.

This additional validation can be a powerful tool for you to use when cleaning up your credit report. Often the credit reporting agencies don't have the needed documentation. This additional requirement can get rid of any illegitimate claims and possibly even legitimate ones—especially older accounts where the records may no longer be easily accessible.

When you send a letter asking a collection agency to validate your account, be sure to send a copy to the credit reporting agencies. This will put them on notice that the item may not be accurate. They, too, will ask for information from the collection agency. If the agency fails to send the information, the item will be removed from your credit report.

Knowing Statutes of Limitations

Up to this point in the chapter I've been discussing credit reports, but there is another set of legal limits you need to understand—the statute of limitations for filing a lawsuit to collect a debt. Creditors can seek a court judgment to collect a debt. If they succeed in getting that judgment, they can then try to collect it by going after your assets or garnishing your wages.

These statutes of limitations vary state by state, but most are 3 to 6 years. Some states allow as much as 15 years for filing a suit for some types of debt.

If a debt is already paid, you don't have to worry about these laws if you want to challenge information on your credit report, but if a debt is unpaid, you could give notice to your creditor that you're planning to fight the debt. That may reawaken their debt-collecting activities and they could decide to file a lawsuit to collect the debt. If you don't plan to repay the debt, you might be better off not questioning the item on your credit report and just let it age until it finally drops off.

If you find that the statute of limitations in your state for filing a lawsuit has already passed, then you can more aggressively question an old debt on your credit file. But seek a legal opinion to be sure that any action you take doesn't restart the clock on the debt and restart the statute of limitations.

Scoring Tips

You can find out the statute of limitations for debts in your state at Consumer Fraud Reporting (www.consumerfraudreporting. org/debtcollectionsol.php). This is an excellent website for finding out many different types of consumer rights.

Generally, for older debt you don't intend to pay, it's best to just let this sleeping dog lie. Yes it will remain for a number of years as a negative mark on your credit report, but renewed collection activities or a lawsuit could be much more costly in many different ways.

You may be wondering whether you should pay the old debt off. That depends on your moral values. A collector can continue to try to collect the debt even after it no longer is reported on your credit report and after the statute of limitations has run out. They won't be able to take you to court, but they can still contact you to collect.

Paying on an old debt can actually hurt your credit score, because the payment will be reported and the date for that item to be removed from your credit report is based on the most recent late payment. Also, in many states, after you make a payment you restart the clock on the statue of limitations, which means the creditor can then take you to court.

But if you have an unpaid debt and you want to get a mortgage on a home, you may have to pay that debt off. Often mortgage companies will not offer a loan to someone with old debts in their credit history. If you want to get a mortgage before that debt is scheduled to drop off your credit report, you probably should pay it off. The sooner you do so the better, so the negative mark can age and your credit score has time

Sometimes you can negotiate with a creditor and tell them you pay the debt off in full, provided they remove the item from your credit report or show the item paid in full without a negative payment history.

Adding Positive Information

The best thing you can do to improve your credit score after a financial crisis is to build on the positive. It's likely that the only type of credit card you'll be able to get at first is a secured credit card. To get that type of card you will have to maintain a savings or checking account with a balance that matches the amount of your credit limit.

Use this card and show that you can be responsible in paying your bills. Be sure to pay your bills on time. Gradually, as more and more positive information is added to your credit report, your score will improve.

Also, be certain that you use your credit cards sparingly. Keep your balances low so the amount of debt shown is only 10 to 20 percent of your credit limit. Even if you pay off your cards every month, the amount you charged will be reported to credit reporting agencies. You can minimize your balance reported by paying the balance due before the end of the period. That way the amount reported to the credit reporting agencies will be $0.

In Chapter 11, I talked more about how to improve your credit score before applying for a loan.

The Least You Need to Know

◆ Negative marks do not stay on your credit report forever. The longest a negative mark can stay on your report is 10 years, and all negatives except Chapter 7 bankruptcy must drop off in 7 years.

◆ Correct errors in paid-off accounts first. Tread carefully if you want to challenge unpaid debts on your credit report.

◆ You can improve your credit score with positive reports. Start using credit again, but use it minimally and pay it off on time.

Part 4

Avoiding Credit Score Mishaps

You probably get information about a credit scam in your e-mail inbox almost every day. Don't fall prey to them. You also need to be concerned about your credit identity. Millions of people find their identities stolen every year. In this part, I explore ways to identify and avoid both credit card scams and credit identity theft. I also discuss your credit rights and how you can use them to protect your credit score.

Chapter 16

Avoiding Credit Score Scams

In This Chapter

- Keeping away from bad fixes
- Requiring it in writing
- Seeking protection after a mistake

You may see an advertisement that looks great after your credit score has been decimated by a credit crisis. The ad screams, "We can erase your bad credit—100% guaranteed."

Don't believe it. Credit repair firms are bad news and may make your situation worse. You may even end up facing legal problems. In this chapter, I talk about the credit repair firms and how they must contract with you legally.

Avoiding Disreputable Credit Fix Firms

If you see an advertisement on TV, radio, or the Internet that promises you ...

- "Credit problems? No problem."

- "We can erase your bad credit—100% guaranteed."

- "Create a new credit identity—legally."

- "We can remove bankruptcies, judgments, and bad loans from your credit file forever!"

Don't believe them and don't pay them any money. Only time and conscientious effort on your part can help you clean up a bad credit history. I talked about how you can do it yourself in Chapters 4 and 15.

Advertising promises such as these can be seen almost daily. These fraudulent firms target consumers nationwide who have poor credit histories. You'll find that they promise to clean up your credit report for a fee. After they finish their work, they promise you'll be able to get a home mortgage, insurance, and a job.

They can't deliver, and you'll just end up throwing away your money. In most cases, they take your money and you never hear from them again.

If you want someone else to do a credit repair for you, there are legitimate firms that will do the work; but before you sign a contract, look for these signs of a disreputable firm:

- If a company wants you to pay for their credit repair services before they provide you any services, don't sign a contract and don't pay them. It's time to walk away from the deal. The Credit Repair Organizations Act requires credit repair companies to complete the promised services before they collect money from you.

- If a company doesn't review your legal rights with you and doesn't tell you what you can do yourself for free, it's the sure sign of a scam.

- If a company tries to dissuade you from contacting a credit reporting agency on your own, they're just trying to get the business. You always have the right to contact a credit reporting agency. I told you how to do so to dispute your credit report in Chapter 4.

- If a company tries to encourage you to invent a new credit history by applying for an *Employer Identification Number* (*EIN*) that you can use instead of your Social Security number, don't even consider doing it unless you operate a viable business that hires employees. It is a federal crime to apply for an EIN fraudulently. It is also a federal crime to apply for credit misrepresenting your Social Security number.

def•i•ni•tion

An **Employer Identification Number (EIN)** is a number for Federal Tax Identification used to identify businesses. You should only apply for this type of number if you are operating a legitimate business and hire employees.

You may think it sounds great to start fresh with a clean credit report using a number other than your own Social Security number. You could end up in jail for fraud. Don't take the risk.

Credit Cautions

You can be charged and prosecuted for mail or wire fraud if you use the mail or telephone to apply for credit and provide false information. This includes lying on a loan or credit application by misrepresenting your Social Security number or using an Employer Identification Number under false pretenses.

Getting Everything in Writing

Before you work with a credit repair company, make sure you get every promise in writing. By law, you must get a copy of the "Consumer Credit File Rights Under State and Federal Law" before you sign a contract with any credit repair company. You can read a copy of this document at www.creditcpr.com/documentation/Your%20Rights.pdf. They must also give you a written contract that spells out your rights.

Even if there is a lot of small print, read every word of the documents you are asked to sign and question anything you don't understand or that isn't clear to you. Don't sign anything until you fully understand it. The law contains protections for you when you contract with a credit repair company. These include the following:

◆ They cannot make false claims about the services they offer.

◆ They cannot ask for money until they have completed the services promised.

◆ They cannot start to do their services for you until you have signed a written contract and they have waited until three days after you signed that contract. You must have a three-day waiting period, during which you can cancel the contract without paying any fees. Don't sign a waiver for these three days. It gives you time to take a closer look at the contract. You may want to use this time to ask a knowledgeable third party or your attorney to review the contract.

The contract itself must also have certain provisions. These required provisions include the following:

◆ The total payment required and the payment terms.

◆ A detailed description of the services to be performed.

◆ The length of time it will take to achieve the results promised.

◆ A detailed list of any guarantees offered.

◆ The company's name and address.

If the contract is missing any of these items, don't sign it. Request that they either provide you with a complete contract or refuse to do business with the company.

Protecting Yourself If You've Already Signed

You may be reading this too late, and you've already contracted with a disreputable credit repair company. Don't hesitate to seek help and report the company. Unfortunately, consumers lose millions of dollars each year to these fraudulent companies.

Scoring Tips

If you're looking for information about repairing your credit report, you can get excellent information for free at the Federal Trade Commission Credit website (www.ftc.gov/credit).

If you have already signed with a disreputable firm, contact your local or state consumer affairs office as quickly as possible. If your state doesn't have a consumer affairs office or the staff member at the consumer affairs office says he can't help you, then call your state's attorney general.

Scoring Tips

You can find your state's consumer action office online at the federal government website Consumer Action (www.consumeraction.gov/state.shtml). In many states, you'll find that the consumer affairs office is part of the state's attorney general's office. If that is not the case, you can find contact information for your state's attorney general at the National Association of Attorneys General website (www.naag.org).

The Least You Need to Know

♦ Any company that promises a 100 percent guarantee to erase your bad credit is a fraud.

♦ Be certain that you get all promises in writing and that you carefully read any contract with a credit repair company before signing it.

♦ If you have already signed a contract with a disreputable firm, don't hesitate to call your state's consumer affairs office or the office of the state's attorney general to ask for help.

Chapter 17

Protecting Your Credit Identity

In This Chapter

♦ Avoiding being exposed

♦ Locking up information

♦ Detecting theft

♦ Fighting back if you're a victim

About 10 million people face identity theft each year, according to the Federal Trade Commission. That's a scary number, and you certainly don't want to be part of it. Your credit score can suffer significantly when an identity thief starts to use your good name.

In this chapter, I give you tips on how to avoid identity theft. I also discuss how you can recover from identity theft if you become a victim.

Defining Identity Theft

Identity theft encompasses any act in which your identity is used fraudulently. You've probably heard of credit card fraud, where someone opens an account in your name or uses your credit card number without your permission. That's what most people think of when they hear identity theft mentioned. In fact, often when a thief starts using your identity, he changes the address on your bills so you don't even know it's happening.

Don't think that credit card fraud is the only type of identity theft. Here are some other common scams:

◆ Phone or utilities fraud: Someone could open an account in your name or run up charges on your existing accounts.

◆ Bank/finance fraud: Someone could open an account in your name and write bad checks. He could find out enough information about you to authorize electronic transfers and drain your savings. He could take out a loan in your name.

◆ Government documents fraud: Someone could get a driver's license or government ID in your name and put his picture on it instead of yours. He could even use your identity to get government benefits or file fraudulent tax returns.

Credit Cautions

If you stop getting your bills, that's a possible sign of identity theft and you should check it out quickly. You also should quickly check out any bills you get for credit cards or loans you did not open yourself. Your credit score can be hurt if you miss paying bills on time.

◆ Your Social Security number could be used on a job application.

◆ A rental contract or medical services could be set up in your name.

◆ Your name could be given to a police officer during an arrest. When you don't show up in court, a warrant could be issued for your arrest.

All these things have happened to people, and it can take years to clear your good name after you are a victim of identity theft. Your best weapon against identity theft is to avoid exposing yourself to it.

Reducing Exposure

Identity theft happens in many different ways. You can reduce your risk by understanding how thieves get hold of your personal data. Here are the most common ways identity thieves get the information they need:

◆ Dumpster diving: They rummage through trash to look for bills or other personal information.

◆ Skimming: They steal your credit card or debit card information by using a special storage device when processing your card.

◆ Phishing: They make you think they are a financial institution or other legitimate company and then ask you to supply your personal information for a loan or other purchase.

◆ Changing your address: They change your address with your credit companies and then get all the information they need mailed directly to them.

◆ Stealing it: They steal your wallet or purse or your mail (to get credit card and bank statements or pre-approved credit offers). They may even get a new box of checks or tax information by stealing your mail. They steal information from their employers or bribe employees who have access to the information to get it.

Often you don't even find out that your identity has been stolen until after the thief has run up thousands of dollars of debt in your name or drained your bank accounts of all the money you had saved.

Securing Your Information

Luckily, with just a little bit of forethought you can secure most of your information against identity theft. You need to change your habits when handling key financial information about yourself. Here are some simple steps you can take:

◆ Shred financial documents and paperwork that have any personal information on them before throwing them out.

◆ Safeguard your Social Security number at all times. Don't carry it in your wallet or print it on your check. If a financial institution, medical insurance company, or anyone else wants to use your

Social Security number as part of your identification number, insist that they use another number.

♦ If you get unsolicited e-mails or even e-mails from what appears to be your bank, don't click on the link. If you think it might be from someone you know, type in the web address that you know before giving out any information. Thieves commonly use phony e-mails to phish for your financial data. Most of these phony e-mails look similar to something official from a bank or government agency.

♦ When you make up your passwords for use on the Internet, don't use information that a thief could find out about you, such as your birth date, your mother's maiden name, your address, or the last four digits of your Social Security number. Develop a random series of numbers and letters and memorize them.

♦ Always keep your personal information in a secure place in your home, especially if you have roommates or employ others who work in your home.

These steps won't guarantee that your information will never be stolen, but thieves usually look for easy targets. The harder you make it for them, the more likely you will deter their success. They will quickly move on to an easier target.

Recognizing the Theft

Even if you do all the right things to protect your identity, a theft can happen. The faster you recognize that you are a victim and act to protect your identity, the less damage your financial history will suffer and the easier it will be to clean up the mess.

If you find that you are a victim of identity theft, act quickly. There are four things you need to do as quickly as possible:

1. Place a fraud alert on your credit reports.

2. Close all accounts.

3. File a police report.

4. Report it to the Federal Trade Commission.

I talk about all these steps in detail in the sections that follow.

Steps You Should Take to Monitor Credit Activity

Monitor your financial accounts frequently and keep tabs on your bill statements. Most financial institutions allow you to access your bank accounts and credit card activity online. Make it a habit to check on activity in those accounts during the month rather than wait for a statement at the end of the month. I recommend that you view your accounts online at least once a week. If you see activity that is not yours, call the financial institution immediately. Most likely they will recommend that you immediately close your account.

You may want to sign up with one of the credit reporting agencies for credit monitoring. They will send you alerts if someone opens a new account in your name. They will also alert you if there is a significant change in an account balance. Credit monitoring can range from $6 to $15 per month.

Possible Signs of Theft

Here are some early signs that your identity may be stolen:

♦ Your bills don't arrive when expected. A thief could have changed your billing address.

♦ You start to receive credit cards or account statements for accounts you know you didn't open yourself.

♦ You are denied credit even though you know you have a good credit history. Anytime you are denied credit, you are given the opportunity to request a free credit report. The information about how to obtain one will be included in the credit denial letter. Immediately call the number given and get a credit report to find out what the problem is.

♦ You get a call or letter about a purchase you didn't make. When you get the call, don't give out any information because it could be a phishing attempt, but do find out as many details about the purchase as you can, as well as the person's name and contact information. Be sure to get the name of the company and then look up a contact number yourself. Call the company after you've checked it out before giving out any information about yourself.

Anytime you suspect a problem with identity theft, you should get a copy of your credit report and be certain you are familiar with all the accounts on that report. In Chapter 3, I introduced you to the parts of a credit report, and in Chapter 4, I told you how to correct any erroneous information.

Placing a Fraud Alert

You can get a fraud alert quickly placed on your credit reports by calling any one of the three credit reporting agencies. They all have toll-free numbers for placing an initial 90-day fraud alert on your credit report. Here are the contact numbers:

- Equifax: 1-800-525-6285
- Experian: 1-888-397-3742 or 1-888-EXPERIAN
- TransUnion: 1-800-680-7289

After you call one of the three agencies, the information will be transmitted to the other two. You will be entitled to free copies of your reports when you place a fraud alert. When you get those reports, look for inquiries from financial institutions, credit card companies, or any other entity that you know you didn't contact yourself. Also look for accounts or loans that you know you didn't open.

When you have a credit alert on your account, you will find it more difficult to open an account while it is there. You will be required to provide additional details about your credit history, including personal data and data about your most recent credit activity on existing accounts.

You may find this very annoying, but it is for your own protection. By requesting the additional information, the creditor hopes to find a possible identity thief before he can open another account. In most cases, an identity thief will not have all the details requested by the financial institution.

Closing Your Accounts

Yes, it's a hassle to change all your account numbers, especially if you have automatic payments set up. But don't hesitate for even a second. When your identity is stolen, you must close your account.

You never know what the identity thief has access to and what his next steps may be. If your wallet or purse was stolen, you'll need to close all accounts that may have been in that wallet or purse. This includes a checking account, if you had checks in there, and all credit cards that were in the purse or wallet.

You should also complete a fraud report with each of the institutions involved. That will protect you from future actions and guarantee that your funds will be returned quickly if additional fraudulent activity is found.

Scoring Tips

The Federal Trade Commission provides an excellent ID Theft Affidavit that you can use to support your written statement. If your financial institution does not have one of its own, you can access it online at ftc.gov/idtheft. You can also file a complaint about identity theft online at that website.

Each financial company will have a security or fraud department that handles these types of calls. In fact, many times when you call a credit card company, you'll hear that one of the options is for reporting a fraud. After you complete the report by phone, the fraud department will likely send you a report that you need to complete in writing. Even if they don't, be sure to back up your call with a letter explaining what you know and sending copies of any proof you have that you are a victim of fraud.

Filing a Police Report

If a significant amount of money is involved, you should report the identity theft to your local law enforcement officials. In many situations, you will need a police report to recover funds lost to theft.

Reporting to the Federal Trade Commission

You should also report any incidence of identity theft to the Federal Trade Commission. They collect information nationally, which helps law enforcement investigations throughout the country. Often this reporting helps them identify a pattern of activity and catch the thieves.

You can report the activity online at ftc.gov/idtheft. If you prefer to contact the FTC by telephone, call 1-800-ID-THEFT (1-800-438-4338). In addition, if you prefer, you can make a report by mail:

Identity Theft Clearinghouse
Federal Trade Commission
Washington, DC 20580

Recovering After Identity Theft

After you've taken the initial steps, you'll then have to go through the arduous task of recovering from the theft. When you file that initial fraud alert, you have the right to a free copy of your credit report. Use it and scour the report for any credit activity or inquiries you don't recognize. If you find things that are not yours, you can ask for an extended alert for up to 12 months that will entitle you to two free credit reports during that 12-month period.

You also have the right to ask for any documentation relating to fraudulent transactions made on your existing accounts or documents that were used to open new accounts. A creditor or other business must give you copies of the applications and other records relating to transactions and accounts that resulted from the theft of your identity. If they refuse your request by telephone, then make it in writing. By law, they cannot refuse to send you a copy of these documents if you request them in writing. A business can require you to send proof of your identity, a police report, and an affidavit before releasing the records.

After you've identified information on your credit report that you believe results from identity theft, you have the right to ask the credit reporting agencies to block that information from your credit file and future credit reports. When you make a request to block information, you must identify the specific information you want blocked. You must also prove your identity and provide the credit reporting agency with an identity theft report.

The credit reporting agency can refuse your request if it believes you didn't provide the necessary information or they believe you made an error or misrepresentation of a material fact. If the credit reporting agency refuses your request, it must notify you.

Scoring Tips

Be sure you can back up your claim by doing your homework in collecting information from the creditors involved. Get a copy of the fraudulent applications and fraudulent credit activity from the businesses or financial institutions so you can make a strong case when reporting the fraud. Also ask for the block with credit reporting agencies.

After a block of the information is in place, a person or business with a block cannot sell, transfer, or place the debt for collection. In addition to obtaining the block, you should also notify the business involved about the identity theft. When notified of an identity theft, the business cannot report any information related to the credit activity you have identified as part of the theft.

Battling identity theft will take a lot of time. You can learn more about how to battle identity theft at www.consumer.gov/idtheft. You can also contact the consumer protection agency or your state's attorney general. You can find your state's consumer action office online at the federal government website Consumer Action (www.consumeraction. gov/state.shtml). In many states, you'll find that the consumer affairs office is part of the state's attorney general's office. If that is not the case, you can find contact information for your state's attorney general at the National Association of Attorneys General website (www.naag. org).

The Least You Need to Know

♦ Identity theft involves more than just the fraudulent use of your credit cards.

♦ You can act to secure your financial information and deter identity thieves.

♦ Be aware of the key warning signs of identity theft, such as not receiving your bills or getting bills for accounts you haven't opened.

♦ Act quickly if you suspect identity theft. The quicker you act, the less damage will be done and the faster you can recover from being an identity theft victim.

Chapter 18

Knowing Your Credit Rights

In This Chapter

- ◆ Discovering your rights
- ◆ Finding out who can help
- ◆ Protecting your rights

Sometimes you may feel as though creditors and credit reporting agencies can do anything they want and not worry about your rights. Luckily, that's not the case. The federal Fair Credit Reporting Act protects you from unscrupulous or uncaring creditors and credit reporting agencies.

In this chapter, I review your rights and tell you who to contact when you believe your rights have been trampled by a creditor or credit reporting agency.

Exploring Your Rights

The accuracy, fairness, and privacy of your credit information are protected by the federal Fair Credit Reporting Act (FCRA). This act protects you from misuse of your information not only by credit reporting agencies, but also by agencies that maintain check writing histories, medical records, and rental history records. Here are your key rights under the FCRA.

Scoring Tips

Reading a copy of any federal law can put almost anyone to sleep, but if you think a creditor or a credit reporting agency has violated your rights, you may want to do further research on what the law says. You can read a copy of the FCRA online at www.ftc.gov/os/statutes/fcradoc.pdf.

No Secrets

If information in your file has been used against you, you must be given notice of that fact. This is true if you're denied credit, denied insurance, or lost a job because of information in a credit file. You must be given the name, address, and phone number of the agency that provides the information. This notice should tell how to get a free copy of your file so you can find out what information was used to make the decision.

Open Door Policy

You must be given access to your file. You have the right to request and obtain all information about you in the files of a credit reporting agency. To get these files you will be asked to provide identification, which likely will include your Social Security number. If the reason you are requesting your file is denial of credit, you should be able to get a free copy of your credit file. Reasons that mandate a free copy of your credit file be provided to you include the following:

◆ You are denied credit, insurance, or a job because of the information in your file. In Chapter 3, I discussed how to read that file, and in Chapter 4, I discussed what you should do to correct any errors you find in that file.

- You are a victim of identity theft and you place a fraud alert on your file. I talked more about identity theft in Chapter 17.

- Your file contains inaccurate information as a result of fraud.

- You are on public assistance.

- You are unemployed, but expect to apply for employment within 60 days.

- You are entitled to one free disclosure of your credit report each year from each of the credit reporting agencies even if none of the above reasons are true.

Getting the Score

You have the right to request your credit score, which creditors use to determine your creditworthiness. I discussed the importance of your credit score and how to get it in Chapter 1.

Scoring Tips

Before you apply for a major loan, such as a mortgage, it is a good idea to check your credit score. The mortgage rate you are offered will depend greatly on that score. Many times when you apply for a mortgage you will be sent a copy of the score used, but that may be too late. As I discussed in Chapter 11, it's important to improve that score before applying for credit.

Disputing Errors

You have the right to dispute any inaccurate or incomplete information. The credit reporting agency must investigate your report and get back to you with details about how they handled your request within 30 days. I discussed how to correct your credit report in Chapter 4.

Removing Information

Credit reporting agencies must correct or delete inaccurate, incomplete, or unverifiable information, usually within 30 days. The consumer reporting agency has the right to continue to report the information you contest if it has verified the information as accurate.

You can attach your side of the story to a report you contest, but that won't impact your credit score. Your explanation will not be taken into consideration when the score is calculated.

Getting Rid of Outdated Information

All credit files have a time limit and outdated information must be removed from your report. A credit reporting agency cannot continue to report information about most negative credit history after it is more than seven years old.

> **Credit Cautions** _____
>
> The only negative mark that can stay on your credit history for more than seven years is a Chapter 7 bankruptcy, which can stay on your report for 10 years. In Chapter 15, I talked about what starts the seven-year clock and what ends it based on the type of credit or creditor.

Accessing Your File

Credit reporting agencies can't send out your information to anyone who requests it. The person requesting your report must have a valid need. Before the credit reporting agency can release the information, they must verify the use of the information. These are the key reasons allowed by law to access your credit file:

- ◆ A court orders that your credit file be released or a subpoena is issued in connection with a federal grand jury.

- ◆ You write to the credit reporting agency and instruct it to release your credit report to an individual or entity.

- ◆ A creditor asks for the report because he intends to use it in connection with a credit transaction or application for credit.

- ◆ An employer intends to use the information for employment purposes. If an employer wants to check your credit file, he must first get your written consent.

- ◆ You applied for a government license that requires the law to consider your financial responsibility or status. For example, if you apply for a real estate license and state law requires a check of your credit history, then your credit file can be released.

◆ The person requesting the file can prove he has a legitimate business reason for requesting the file.

◆ A child support enforcement agency can request your credit file when considering a person's ability to pay. You must be given a 10-day notice of the intention to request your report before it is requested. The report can only be used to determine ability to pay and appropriate levels of those payments. The information cannot be used in any other civil, administrative, or criminal proceeding.

Limiting Offers

Are you tired of getting all those unsolicited credit offers? You have the right to remove your name and address from prescreened credit and insurance lists. To stop getting all that annoying mail or those annoying telephone calls about available credit or insurance, opt out by calling 1-888-5-OPTOUT (1-888-567-8688).

Seeking Damages

If you believe your rights have been violated, you have the right to sue the violator in state or federal court. Damages up to $1,000 plus attorney's fees can be awarded if the court finds in your favor.

Scoring Tips

People who are victims of identity theft or active military personnel have additional rights. I discussed the additional rights for victims of identity theft in Chapter 17. To find out more about active duty alerts for military personnel, go to www.ftc.gov/bcp/conline/pubs/alerts/dutyalrt.htm.

Introducing Key Agencies

You can get help from both your state and the federal government if you believe your rights have been transgressed. Some states offer more extensive protection than the federal government, so it's a good idea to talk with your state consumer action office first. You can find your state's consumer action office online at the federal government website Consumer Action (www.consumeraction.gov/state.shtml).

Scoring Tips

If you want to report fraud or seek the state's legal assistance because you believe your credit rights have been violated, contact your state's attorney general's office. You can find a contact for your state's attorney general at the National Association of Attorneys General website (www.naag.org).

The federal agency you'll need to contact will depend on the type of financial institution or other entity involved in your complaint. The key contact points include the following:

Consumer reporting agencies, creditors, and any others not found in the following list.

Federal Trade Commission
Consumer Response Center—
FCRA
Washington, DC 20580
1-877-382-4357

National banks and federal branches/agencies of foreign banks. You'll find "National" or "N.A." in or after the bank's name.

Office of the Comptroller of the Currency
Compliance Management, Mail Stop 6-6
Washington, DC 20219
1-800-613-6743

Federal Reserve System member banks except national banks or federal branches/agencies of foreign banks.

Federal Reserve Board
Division of Consumer & Community Affairs
Washington, DC 20551
1-202-452-3693

Savings associations and federally charted savings banks. You'll find the word "federal" or initials F.S.B. in the bank names.

Office of Thrift Supervision
Consumer Complaints
Washington, DC 20552
1-800-842-6929

Federal credit unions.

National Credit Union Administration
1775 Duke Street
Alexandria, VA 22314
1-703-519-4600

State-chartered banks that are not members of the Federal
Reserve System.

Federal Deposit Insurance Corporation
Consumer Response Center
2345 Grand Avenue, Suite 100
Kansas City, MO 64108
1-877-275-3342

Air, surface, or rail carriers regulated by the Interstate Commerce
Commission.

Department of Transportation
Office of Financial Management
Washington, DC 20590
1-202-366-1306

Taking Steps to Protect Your Rights

You're the only one who can protect your rights. No one will watch out
for your rights, so you need to get to know your credit report and correct any errors.

Be aware of your rights to access your report, and know the people
who can also legitimately do so. I've summarized those rights in this
chapter, but you can get more information about the FCRA at www.ftc.
gov/credit.

Don't hesitate to call your state's consumer action center if you have
any questions, or call the Federal Trade Commission. Protect your
rights and your credit score to get the best interest rates when applying
for credit.

The Least You Need to Know

- ◆ Your credit identity is not a free-for-all. You can seek protection for your credit privacy based on regulations of the Fair Credit Reporting Act.

- ◆ Some states offer better protection than the federal government, so call your state consumer action office first. The federal agency that you need to contact depends on the type of financial institution or other entity involved.

- ◆ You need to be proactive about protecting your credit history and credit score. No one will do that for you.

Glossary

charge back—This is the process for disputing charges to your credit card bill. You must dispute a charge on your bill within 60 days after you receive the bill or you will not be able to use the charge back process.

charge off—This means that the creditor wrote off the account to bad debt and does not expect you will ever pay the money.

credit counseling—This is a process where counselors, who specialize in negotiating lower interest rates, work out payment plans with your creditors to help get you out of debt. The plans they work out are called debt management plans.

credit inquiries—This includes any request by a third party to look at your credit report. There are two types of inquiries—hard and soft. A hard inquiry is one based on an application you filled out when applying for credit. A soft inquiry is one where a creditor looks at your file possibly to offer you a new credit card or to look at the credit history of current customers.

credit tradelines—This includes details about a specific credit account. For example, if you had an account with Citigroup, your credit tradeline would include all the account information about that specific credit card, including your credit limit and your payment history.

debt management plan—This is a systematic way to pay down your debt. You need to have enough income to make the payments for a debt management plan to work.

debt utilization ratio—This looks at the amount of your debt versus the amount of available credit. It is calculated using this formula: debt/ total credit.

foreclosure—This is the process in which the financial institution that offered you a mortgage on your home takes possession of the home for failure to make the mortgage payments.

installment accounts—This includes car and furniture loans. These are accounts where you agree to pay a specific amount over a specific period of time until the full balance is paid off.

mortgage accounts—This includes any loan in which you put your house up as collateral, which means the lender can take your property if you don't pay the loan.

overdraft/reserve checking accounts—These are accounts where the bank automatically draws from your allowable credit if you write a check for more than your balance. These types of accounts allow you to avoid overdraft fees on checks.

quit-claim—This deed transfers the ownership of a property. Essentially, if you quit-claim the deed on your house to your spouse, you are giving up your title to that property.

repossession—This is the process by which the financial institution that financed your car takes possession of the car for failure to pay the monthly amount due.

revolving account—This includes credit card accounts and retail store accounts. Essentially, these are accounts where your balance due can go up and down depending on how much you charge.

secured debt—This is debt that is secured by assets, such as a mortgage on your house or a loan on your car. If you fail to pay a secured debt, you can lose the asset that was put up as collateral. For example, you can lose a home to foreclosure if you fail to pay the mortgage, and you can lose a car to repossession if you fail to pay a car loan.

"subprime" borrower—This is someone who has less than perfect credit. A bankruptcy definitely puts you in this category, but you can also end up there if you have a lot of late payments, repossession (major item taken back for nonpayment), or a foreclosure (house taken back by lender) on your record. "Subprime" borrowers pay interest rates that are at least 5 to 10 percent higher than borrowers with a better score.

unsecured debt—This is debt that has not been secured by assets. This includes credit cards and personal loans.

usury laws—These protect the public from the charging of unreasonable or relatively high interest rates. The word comes from the Medieval Latin word *usuria*, which means "interest" or "excessive interest."

Appendix B

Resources

Government Agencies

Federal Trade Commission. The federal agency responsible for helping you protect your credit rights is the Federal Trade Commission (www.ftc.gov).

If you're looking for information about repairing your credit report, you can get excellent information for free at the Federal Trade Commission Credit website (www.ftc.gov/credit).

Battling identity theft will take a lot of time. You can learn more about it at www.consumer.gov/idtheft.

You can report any fraudulent activity online at ftc.gov/idtheft. If you prefer to contact the FTC by telephone, call 1-800-ID-THEFT (1-800-438-4338). If you prefer, you can also make a report by mail:

Identity Theft Clearinghouse
Federal Trade Commission
Washington, DC 20580

You can read a copy of the Federal Credit Reporting Act online at www.ftc.gov/os/statutes/fcradoc.pdf. If you are a member of the military, find out more about your rights when on active duty at www.ftc.gov/bcp/conline/pubs/alerts/dutyalrt.htm.

OPTOUT. Are you tired of getting all those unsolicited credit offers? You have the right to remove your name and address from prescreened credit and insurance lists. To stop getting all that annoying mail or those annoying telephone calls about available credit or insurance, opt out by calling 1-888-5-OPTOUT (1-888-567-8688).

Reporting Credit Complaints. You must report any credit complaints to the proper federal agency. Here are the key contacts:

Consumer reporting agencies, creditors, and any others not found in the following list.

> Federal Trade Commission
> Consumer Response Center—FCRA
> Washington, DC 20580
> 1-877-382-4357

National banks, federal branches/agencies of foreign banks. You'll find "National" or "N.A." in or after the bank's name.

> Office of the Comptroller of the Currency
> Compliance Management, Mail Stop 6-6
> Washington, DC 20219
> 1-800-613-6743

Federal Reserve System member banks, except national banks or federal branches/agencies of foreign banks.

> Federal Reserve Board
> Division of Consumer & Community Affairs
> Washington, DC 20551
> 1-202-452-3693

Savings associations and federally charted savings banks. You'll find the word "federal" or initials F.S.B. in the bank names.

> Office of Thrift Supervision
> Consumer Complaints
> Washington, DC 20552
> 1-800-842-6929

Federal credit unions.

> National Credit Union Administration
> 1775 Duke Street
> Alexandria, VA 22314
> 1-703-519-4600

State-chartered banks that are not members of the Federal Reserve System.

> Federal Deposit Insurance Corporation
> Consumer Response Center
> 2345 Grand Avenue, Suite 100
> Kansas City, MO 64108
> 1-877-275-3342

Air, surface, or rail carriers regulated by the Interstate Commerce Commission.

> Department of Transportation
> Office of Financial Management
> Washington, DC 20590
> 1-202-366-1306

State Consumer Action Offices. Sometimes you can get more protection from your state. You can find your state's consumer action office online at the federal government website Consumer Action (www.consumeraction.gov/state.shtml). In many states you'll find that the consumer affairs office is part of the state's attorney general's office.

State Attorney General. You can find a contact for your state's attorney general at the National Association of Attorneys General (www.naag.org).

Credit Reporting Agencies

Free Credit Report. You can get a free copy of your credit report at www.annualcreditreport.com/cra/index.jsp. Don't use any other website if you want a free copy of your credit report. All the others will sign you up for credit monitoring services you may not want. You are entitled to one free credit report each year.

Credit Score. You can get a copy of your credit score at www.myfico. com. You have to pay for your credit score, however. Through myFICO you can order all three scores from the three key credit reporting agencies—Equifax, Experian, and TransUnion.

Credit Reporting Agency Websites. For Equifax, it's www.econsumer. equifax.com. For Experian, it's www.experian.com/identity_fraud. For TransUnion, it's www.truecredit.com.

Call to Report Credit Fraud

You can get a fraud alert quickly placed on your credit reports by calling any one of the three credit reporting agencies. They all have toll-free numbers for placing an initial 90-day fraud alert on your credit report. Here are the contact numbers:

Equifax: 1-800-525-6285

Experian: 1-888-397-3742 or 1-888-EXPERIAN

TransUnion: 1-800-680-7289

Credit Scores and Interest Rates. Fair Isaac has an excellent calculator you can use to view today's interest rates based on credit scores and how your payments will be impacted. You can input your loan amounts and the calculator will automatically calculate the differences based on your credit score. You can try out this calculator at www.myfico.com/ myfico/CreditCentral/LoanRates.asp.

Consumer Credit Information Websites

Living Frugally. You'll find lots of ideas about how to live more frugally at the Frugal Life (www.thefrugallife.com).

Debt Reduction. An excellent tool you can access online to help you develop a repayment plan is the Debt Reduction Planner at Quicken. com (www.quicken.com/planning/debt). Use this tool to help you sort out your debt and come up with a repayment plan. CNN also offers a debt reduction planner that is easy to use at http://cgi.money.cnn.com/ tools/debtplanner/debtplanner.jsp.

Consumer Fraud Reporting

To find out more about consumer fraud and consumer rights, visit www.consumerfraudreporting.org.

Credit Counseling

National Foundation for Credit Counselors. Find certified and accredited counselors at www.nfcc.org. They also operate an excellent consumer website at www.debtadvice.org, where you can find out more about credit counseling services and how to pick the right counselor.

HUD Housing Counselors. If your home is financed through the FHA, seek the help of a U.S. Department of Housing and Urban Development housing counselor. You can find one near your home by searching its database online at www.hud.gov/offices/hsg/sfh/hcc/hcs.cfm, or call 1-800-333-4636 to find an office near you. HUD housing counselors can help you with credit counseling, and in many cases their services are free. They will definitely work to help you keep your house.

Bankruptcy Approved Counselors. You must seek credit counseling before applying for bankruptcy. You can find out more about credit counseling and the approved agencies at the U.S. Trustee website (www.usdoj.gov/ust/eo/bapcpa/ccde/index.htm).

Bankruptcy

Bankruptcy Attorneys. You can find bankruptcies in your area online at the National Association of Consumer Bankruptcy Attorneys (www.nacba.org). When you get to the home page, click the top right link titled "Attorney Finder."

If you need free help, you can find a state-by-state directory at the Legal Services Corporation website (www.lsc.gov). When you get to the website, look for a link at the top right called "Find Legal Assistance."

Bankruptcy Trustee. You can find out more about the U.S. Bankruptcy Court and the U.S. Trustee Program at www.usdoj.gov/ust/index.htm. You can also find links for all the forms you need to file for bankruptcy at that website.

Personal Bankruptcy Information. You can find out about the rules for personal bankruptcy and exemptions in your state at www.bankruptcyinformation.com/services.html.

Appendix C

Sample Letters

Here are sample letters you can use in various situations when trying to correct a credit problem. Be sure you always keep a copy of your letter and attach any follow-up letters to that copy in case a question about the situation arises again in the future. A good paper trail can be your best defense in any credit dispute. Telephone calls will not protect you.

Correcting Inaccurate Information on Your Credit Report

Use this sample letter format when you want to correct information on your credit report:

Date
Your Name
Your Address
Your City, State, Zip Code

Customer Service
Name of Company
Address City, State, Zip Code

Dear Sir or Madam:

I am writing to dispute the following information in my credit file. The items I dispute also are circled on the attached copy of the report I received.

PROBLEM 1

If the item in question is inaccurate, use this paragraph:

"This item (identify item[s] disputed by name of source and account number and identify type of item, such as credit account, judgment, and so on) is inaccurate because (describe what is inaccurate and why—such as inaccurately states I missed the payment of [give date])."

PROBLEM 2

If the item in question is incomplete, use this paragraph:

"This item (identify item[s] disputed by name of source and account number and identify type of item, such as credit account, judgment, and so on) is incomplete because (describe what is incomplete and why, such as is missing my credit limit of $_____)."

PROBLEM 3

If the item in question should not be in your credit file, use this paragraph:

"This item (identify item[s] disputed by name of source and account and identify type of item, such as credit account, judgment, and so on) should be deleted because (describe why, such as this is not my debt or the item is more than seven years old)."

Finish all letters with the following closing:

Enclosed are copies of (describe any enclosed documentation, such as payment records, court documents) supporting my position. Please investigate this (these) matter(s) and (delete or correct) the disputed item(s) as soon as possible.

Sincerely,

Your Name

Enclosures: (*List what you are enclosing.*)

Correcting Inaccurate Billing

Use this letter if you need to correct inaccurate billing:

Date
Your Name
Your Address
Your City, State, Zip Code

Customer Service
Name of Company
Address
City, State, Zip Code

RE: Name, Account Number

Dear Sir or Madam:

On my statement of (give date), I saw a charge for $_____ from (give company). The charge is not correct because (explain what is incorrect about the charge). (*If you have an attachment to prove your dispute, then attach a copy and add something such as:* "The attached receipt will show you the correct bill amount.") Please send acknowledgement of this letter within 30 days or correct my account prior to that time. You must complete correction of this error within two billing cycles or explain to me why you believe the item billed is correct.

Sincerely,

Your Name

Enclosure: (*Describe enclosure if you have one.*)

Letter to Freeze Credit in a Divorce Situation

Use this letter as soon as possible after starting the process of divorce. You should send this letter to all your creditors:

Date
Your Name
Your Address
Your City, State, Zip Code

Customer Service
Name of Company
Address
City, State, Zip Code

Dear Sir or Madam:

I am writing to alert you to the fact that my husband or wife (give name) and I are getting divorced. I am requesting that you freeze our credit account(s) (list all accounts you want frozen).

I will not be responsible for any transactions charged to these accounts after (give date).

Sincerely,

Your Name

Notification of Disputed Item Form— Citicorp

Some companies provide you the ability to dispute an item on your bill online. Here is a sample of Citicorp's online dispute form:

Notification of Disputed Item   Thursday, February 8, 2007

Please call Customer Service prior to completing this form. 1-800-950-5114.

Complete this form online, **PRINT**, sign and mail it to the Customer Service address below.
Do not mail this form with your payment. Do not use this form if your card has been lost, stolen or you have not received it; call Customer Service immediately.

Case ID:

Name:

Signature:

              Date:

Account #:

              Amount of Dispute:$

Virtual Account #:

Reference #:

Merchant:

I have examined the charges made to my account and I am disputing an item for the following reason:

(1) ○ Neither I nor any person authorized by me to use my card made the charge listed above. In addition, neither I nor anyone authorized by me received the goods and services represented by this transaction. **(If you do not recognize a sale, choose this option and call Customer Service immediately.)**

(2) ○ Although I did participate in a transaction with the merchant, I was billed for   transaction(s) totaling $
        that I did not engage in, nor did anyone else authorized to use my card. I do have all of my cards in my possession. **Enclosed is a copy of the authorized sales slip.**

(3) ○ I have not received the merchandise that was to have been shipped to me. Expected date of delivery was   (mm-dd-yy). I contacted the merchant on   (mm-dd-yy), and the merchant's response was

                         (In order to assist you, the merchant must be contacted.)

(4) ○ I have (select one) ☐ returned ☐ canceled the merchandise on   (mm-dd-yy) because

(Please provide a copy of the returned receipt, postal receipt or proof of refund.)

(5) ○ The attached credit slip was listed as a charge on my statement.

(6) ○ I was issued a credit slip for $ on   (mm-dd-yy), which was not shown on my monthly statement. **A copy of my credit slip is enclosed.**

(7) ○ Merchandise that was shipped to me arrived damaged and/or defective on   (mm-dd-yy). I returned it on   (mm-dd-yy). Merchant's response was

(Please provide postal receipt and/or credit slip.)

(8) ○ My account was charged $ but I should have been billed $ **Enclosed is a copy of the sales receipt and/or other documents which indicate the correct amount.**

(9) ○ **Other** - Attach a letter describing the dispute.

Complete this form, Print
and Mail to:
                    P.O. Box 6035
                    The Lakes, NV 89163-6035

Ask Collection Agency to Validate Your Debt

If you find a collection agency collection action on your credit report that you believe is not accurate, then you should write the collection agency, as well as the credit reporting agency. Here is a sample of the letter. If you receive a letter from a collection agency and you question the debt, you must send a request to validate the date within 30 days:

Date
Your Name
Your Address
Your City, State, Zip Code

Contact Name or Collector
Name of Company
Address
City, State, Zip Code

Dear Contact Name or Collector:

> Use this paragraph if you saw the debt on your credit file:

> "I'm in receipt of a credit report from (name company) concerning (give details about debt that you have). I dispute this debt. Please send validation."

> Use this paragraph if you received a debt collection letter:

> "I'm in receipt of your collection notice dated (give date) concerning (name company and account number). I dispute this debt. Please send validation."

Sincerely,

Your Name

Index